BRAVE
the
PAGE

BRAVE
the
PAGE

A Young Writer's Guide to Telling Epic Stories

By Rebecca Stern & Grant Faulkner

NANOWRIMO

VIKING

VIKING

An imprint of Penguin Random House LLC, New York

First published in the United States of America by Viking,
an imprint of Penguin Random House LLC, 2019

Visit us online at penguinrandomhouse.com

LIBRARY OF CONGRESS CATALOGING-IN-PUBLICATION DATA IS AVAILABLE
ISBN 9780451480293

Printed in U.S.A.   Set in Ionic MT Pro   Book design by Nancy Brennan

1 3 5 7 9 10 8 6 4 2

CONTENTS

✖

WARNING: Following the advice in this book will lead you toward achieving big things. You'll write more—and faster—than you've ever written before. Your imagination will get bigger and stronger. You'll be more confident and take more risks. By the end of your writing adventure, you will be a different person. Don't believe it? We dare you to prove us wrong.

INTRODUCTION
by Jason Reynolds

Okay.

You're here.

I suspect that means you're interested in writing a novel. I know a little (just a little) about writing novels, but I'm going to be completely honest with you: I'm writing this introduction lying on a couch in the weird new house I just bought, because, for me, today was moving day. Meaning, a few hours ago I moved from an apartment to a house, and the last thing on my mind is talking about novels, because it's really hard to think about stories when you're drenched in sweat and covered in whatever kind of sneezy dust-pepper that cardboard boxes seem to make infinite amounts of.

Like I said, I know a little (just a little) about

writing novels. However, after today, I feel like I know *much* more about moving. About somehow packing life into boxes. My clothes and shoes (so many pairs of shoes!). My books. The ones on the shelf. The ones next to the bed. The ones stacked along the walls. All of them had to be packed away. My dresser, and bed, and sofa, and chairs. Pots and pans. Plates and glasses. Spoons, forks, and knives (oh my!). And also all the things I've collected—my trinkets and tchotchkes. Silly childhood photos. My grandfather's cookie jar. Coins I've saved from around the world. And most importantly, letters from readers I've received over the years. All packed up in boxes. *A whole lot of boxes.* Taped and labeled like mummies with tattoos.

I wish I could tell you the fun stopped there. But it didn't.

After the packing came the loading. Those 200 boxes (and when I say 200, I mean somewhere around 40) had to be carried down the 15 steps leading to the door of my building, through that door, down the stoop, through the gate, and into the truck. We had to take the legs off the sofa so we could maneuver it, tilting it, wiggling it through the narrow doorway and down the stairwell. And the bed . . . you don't even want to know!

After the loading came driving to the new place, and once we finally arrived, we had to unload everything. The thought of it all made me question if maybe I could just live in the truck. I mean, my bed was already there, and so was my sofa. I figured it could be kind of cozy, but the winter nights might get tricky, so . . . onward with the unloading we went. Box after box taken from the back of the truck, carried up the 20 steps leading to the front door. The sofa and bed had to be moved strategically again. And the boxes of my memories and mementos—labeled FRAGILE—were moved gently and placed in corners, clear of leaning (and eventually falling) mattresses.

And right now, as I write this, I'm looking over my laptop screen at all the boxes in this new place, shaking my head because tomorrow I'll have to unpack. I'll have to figure out where my things belong in this home. Where do the books go? And what about the art, and the letters? My family pictures? Where does the sofa belong? And what about my bed? Also, I need to buy curtains. Immediately. And I hope I packed what was left of the toilet paper, but even if I did, it's going to take me *forever* to find it. *Oof.* Smells like paint in here. Speaking of paint, I'm pretty sure I put a small hole in the wall moving my dresser. My new wall. Oh well, I guess that makes it mine now.

I'm rambling.

But I'm not. See, I know a little (just a little) about writing novels, and what I can tell you is that the process is exactly like moving from one home to the next. Your characters are your boxes. The protagonist is, perhaps, the biggest box, packed with a little bit of this, a little bit of that: dirty shoes, random books, and *always* some of the fragile stuff as well. Your job is to take them from a familiar place, a place where they feel they belong, and get them to the truck. Sometimes that means forcing them through the door, removing legs, bending a corner of the box. Sometimes that means sliding them down the steps, letting them tumble and burst open. Sometimes that means taking them through the back door and walking them through the alley.

And once you've got them in the truck, you have to take them on the journey that gets them from one place to the next. It may be dark, it may be bumpy, and there may even be traffic—stop and go, stop and go—the boxes uncontrollably slamming against each other.

Then, upon arrival, you have to get them from the truck, up even more steps than they'd come down when leaving their home, and somehow get them inside. Again, this may take maneuvering, and the boxes might be damaged in the process. But once you're through the door—the *new* door—those boxes will be sitting in a much bigger, more beautiful space. And you're thinking, *Yes, I did it!* But the truth is, now that big box—and all the special things in it—has to find its place all over again. It has survived the journey, but now must figure out where it belongs in this spacious—though . . . weird—new environment.

Pack, load, journey, unload, unpack. That's a novel. And guess what? It's *you* lifting the boxes. You will sweat. You'll get dirty. You'll even try to convince yourself to let the boxes stay in the truck. And when that happens, use this book as your dolly (the strange little metal thing with wheels that people use to move heavy boxes).

And if it ever gets *really* tough, return to this introduction. Take a deep breath. Then read and remember the first (or last) three words.

Okay.

You're home.

....

JASON REYNOLDS is a *New York Times* bestselling author, a Newbery Award Honoree, a Printz Award Honoree, a National Book Award Honoree, a Kirkus Prize winner, a two-time Walter Dean Myers Award winner, an NAACP Image Award winner, and the recipient of multiple Coretta Scott King Honors. The American Booksellers Association's 2017 spokesperson for Indies First, he has written many books including *When I Was the Greatest*, *The Boy in the Black Suit*, *All American Boys* (cowritten with Brendan Kiely), *As Brave as You*, *For Every One*, the Track series (*Ghost*, *Patina*, *Sunny*, and *Lu*), and *Long Way Down*, which received both a Newbery Honor and a Printz Honor. He lives in Washington, DC. You can find his ramblings at JasonWritesBooks.com.

THE WORLD NEEDS YOUR STORY

The world is made up of protons, neutrons, electrons—and stories. Everything you see, touch, hear, taste, and smell is a story. We breathe stories in and breathe them out. We swim through oceans of them without ever getting tired. If you distill a lifetime, you're left with a story.

Stories let us live infinite lives. They let us walk in the shoes of a person who lives thousands of miles away and experience things that otherwise wouldn't be possible. Stories shift our thinking and expand our worlds. They connect us and make us more empathetic. They show us we're not alone. Through stories, we're able to fly far away to distant lands, and also into the depths of ourselves.

The Story of You started the moment you entered the world (or maybe even before then) and is made up of millions of little stories strung together like holiday lights across the span of your lifetime. Some of these stories are fleeting and fast and happen every second of every day; they are only flickers. These stories are just you being you: walking from your first class to your second, wrestling with your dog after school, giving your grandmother a hug.

Other stories are bigger, stickier; you remember them vividly—like when you won your first gold medal in a swim meet and had your picture taken for the local newspaper, or the time your brother pulled your hair and then told your mother that *you* were the one who pulled *his* hair and you watched incredulously as his crocodile tears poured from his eyes and your mother, despite your protests, sent you to your room to "think about what you've done."

Here's the thing about the Story of You: You are the only one who has lived your life. Your experiences are unique because they are yours. Your stories are important because they are your stories. And the stories you tell—whether fact or fiction— can only be told by you.

Your stories will help people who are different from you understand your experience. And for people with similar backgrounds, your stories will say, "I see you. I get you. You are not alone."

Your stories matter, and the world needs them.

WELCOME TO NANOWRIMO

> NaNoWriMo helped me realize what I'm capable of as a writer, and it helped me learn how to set and achieve goals. I feel more confident in my writing skills (and a little more braggy). —Tanya, a Young Writers Program participant, 2016

Throughout the month of November, if you stop what you're doing, tilt your head to the sky, and listen really hard, you'll hear this: *clickety-click, clickety-click, tap tap tap, tap tap tap*. What are these sounds? They're stories being born. Every year, on November 1, nearly 500,000 people (including more than 100,000 kids and educators) set out to do something extraordinary: draft an entire novel from scratch in just 30 days.

Over the course of National Novel Writing

Month (NaNoWriMo), these intrepid writers fly across the page at record speeds, giving life to new characters and creating entire landscapes using nothing more than their imaginations. They live and breathe their stories. They wake up in the morning and eat plot twists for breakfast. They brush their teeth using their characters' toothpaste. Every day, they write word after word after word after word, until they reach "The End."

....

NANOWRIMO (pronounced *na-noh-rye-mo*) has been helping people hurdle over the blank page to tell the stories that matter to them since 1999. Our three main programs—National Novel Writing Month, the Young Writers Program (YWP), and Camp NaNoWriMo—give participants the tools and resources they need to accomplish big things, like writing a novel in 30 days, and empower people of all ages and from all backgrounds to tell the stories that matter to them.

WHO SHOULD READ
BRAVE THE PAGE?

If you are a young writer who wants to tackle big creative writing projects, like drafting a novel in a month or a short story in a week, *Brave the Page* is for you. If you love to write but don't think you're good at it, *Brave the Page* is for you. If you love to write and think you're a fantastic writer, *Brave the Page* is for you. Whoever you are, wherever you live, and whatever your creative aspirations, this book is for you.

Brave the Page will guide you through the NaNoWriMo writing process, and will:

>> Teach you how to set yourself up for success by creating a goal and a deadline for your writing project.

>> Guide you through the prewriting stage so that you are fully prepared to hit the blank page with a running start on day one. You'll learn how to develop characters, build worlds, and collect plot ideas.

>> Keep you on track during your writing project with a week-by-week map that includes strategies and tried-and-true wisdom, as well as ways to enrich your story and write through writer's block.

>> Answer the question "What's next?" by showing you how to move beyond your draft and into the revision and editing stages, and how to create a year-round writing habit.

On the Young Writers Program website (ywp. nanowrimo.org), participants have access to a magical device called the Dare Machine, which pumps out prompts and inspiration. You'll find the Dare Machine here, in *Brave the Page*, as well. In Part 1, the Dare Machine will help you set yourself up for success; in Part 2, it will help you develop characters, create settings, and figure out a plot so that you have a complete plan for a story; and in Part 3, it will give you inspiration and ideas to help move your story forward.

1
GET READY

Cozy up around our imaginary campfire, help yourself to some s'mores, and learn how to get ready for your writing adventure. In Part 1, you'll set yourself up for success by learning how to find story ideas, make a deadline, set a goal, and create a routine.

WHERE STORY IDEAS COME FROM

There's this Shel Silverstein poem about a girl, Jane, who, because she's very thirsty, waits (and waits and waits) with her mouth open for it to rain. It's a very funny poem. Can you imagine choosing to wait with your mouth open for an indeterminate amount of time rather than immediately quenching your thirst by grabbing a glass of water?

The poem is called "Lazy Jane." It's easy to laugh at Jane's foolishness, but a lot of writers—whether they realize it or not—end up doing exactly what she's doing, only they're not waiting for it to rain; they're waiting (and waiting and waiting) for inspiration to fall from the sky. They haven't realized (yet) that they're sitting right next to an unending supply of story ideas—and that it only takes a little effort to recognize them.

The most common question authors get asked is, "How do you come up with your ideas?" People ask this because they're curious, but also because they have a hope that the author answering the question will lean in real close and whisper something like, "I'm not supposed to tell you this, but all you have to do to get an *awesome* story idea is blink three times, rub your belly counterclockwise, and sneeze under a blanket!" But alas, this is never the answer because *there isn't a secret formula for cooking up story ideas.*

So if you shouldn't wait for ideas to fall from the sky, and there isn't a secret formula to conjure them up, what *can* you do to find them? Where does inspiration come from?

"You get ideas from daydreaming. You get ideas from being bored," *Coraline* author Neil Gaiman wrote. "The only difference between writers and other people is we notice when we're doing it."

The truth is, story ideas are flittering and flapping and zipping and zapping all around us, all the time. They're carved in the pavement and etched in our memories and painted on the sides of buildings. They're stuck under our desks like wads of gum and buried in the early-morning news. They're hidden in our secrets and lingering around our friendships. Really, they're everywhere.

This isn't to say that grabbing hold of an idea is easy—they can be slippery and sly and fleeting!—but once you know they're all around you, you can set out to catch them using various idea-catching mechanisms. (We recommend having a notebook handy at all times for jotting down captured ideas, too.) You're not only a writer, after all; you're also a story collector.

Idea-Catching Mechanisms

● MINE YOUR LIFE

When you *mine* your life, you look back through your past to extract sparkling sapphires as well as pieces of combustible coal. You dig deep to uncover experiences and emotions and memories and dreams, and then you gather them in a pile and watch as they ignite and spark story ideas.

The nuggets you mine from your past don't need to be *epic* or *amazing* or *tragic* (though they can be). They can be simple moments or heated conversations or the smell of your favorite holiday. It can be that time when you were three years old and used your mom's lipstick as a crayon on the freshly painted wall. Or that feeling you got when you aced (or failed) your math test. Or the color of the sky after you saw your grandfather for the last time.

Your memories might lead to wild new ideas. Or they might serve as a foundation upon which you build your story, as with author Joyce Hansen's book *The Gift-Giver*, which came out of her past experiences. "I recalled my own childhood as I created the story, so that underneath what seems to be a contemporary middle-grade novel is actually a nostalgic memory of my years growing up in a Bronx neighborhood in the late 1940s and early '50s."

To get started on mining your life, take 10 minutes to write down (or draw) as many memories, experiences, and dreams as you can. Include a lot of details or a single word—whatever works for you. Do this every day for a week.

Here are a few prompts to guide you if mining memories from your whole life feels too big:

>> **MONDAY:** Holidays or special gatherings

>> **TUESDAY:** A time you tried something new

>> **WEDNESDAY:** School events or field trips

>> **THURSDAY:** A time that was particularly funny, happy, or sad

>> **FRIDAY:** Family members or pets

>> **SATURDAY:** A time you were scared or embarrassed

>> **SUNDAY:** Your earliest memory

⊕ LISTS

Because we think of making lists for Christmas or birthdays or grocery shopping, this may seem like an odd activity at first, but lists are also a great way to trigger ideas for stories. As you add items to your list, you'll begin to dip into your subconscious (that wonderful, dreamlike place in your mind that is difficult to enter), leading you to great fodder for your writing adventures.

Fahrenheit 451 author Ray Bradbury used this technique to generate ideas for his stories (as well as for story titles). He'd make long lists of whatever nouns popped into his head, letting each word lead to the next.

For Bradbury, this type of word association ultimately uncovered long-forgotten places and people and memories and feelings and *stories*. He said, "These lists were the provocations, finally, that caused my better stuff to surface. I was feeling my way toward something honest, hidden under the trapdoor on the top of my skull."

Here's what one of his lists looked like:

"THE LAKE. THE NIGHT. THE CRICKETS.
THE RAVINE. THE ATTIC. THE BASEMENT.
THE TRAPDOOR. THE BABY. THE CROWD.
THE NIGHT TRAIN. THE FOG HORN. THE
SCYTHE. THE CARNIVAL. THE CAROUSEL.
THE DWARF. THE MIRROR MAZE. THE
SKELETON."

When he was done with a list, he'd pick one of the words and "sit down to write a long prose-poem-essay on it." Sometimes a word would lead to an entire story; other times a word would lead to another word, which would lead to a title, which would lead to a story.

What happened to the list above? It led to his novel *Something Wicked This Way Comes*.

So what should you make a list of? Anything and everything! Here are some ideas to get you started:

 Things that make you mad or happy (or make you feel any other emotion)

 Memories

Things that make you laugh

 Places you've visited or want to visit

 Things you do every day

Keep your lists in your notebook and add to them often—even if a particular list doesn't spark a story right now, it may later!

OPPOSITES OR WILDLY DIFFERENT ELEMENTS

What happens when you combine reality TV and war footage? You get *The Hunger Games*. When asked how she came up with the idea for the book, Suzanne Collins said, "One night, I was lying in bed and I was very tired and I was just sort of channel surfing on television. And I was going through, flipping through images of reality television where there were these young people competing for a million dollars or a bachelor or whatever. And then I was flipping and I was seeing footage from the Iraq War. And these two things began to sort of fuse together in a very unsettling way, and that . . . I think was the moment where I got the idea for Katniss's story."

To find wildly different things to combine, you could:

>> Take a historical figure (that is, someone who made a mark on history and has been dead for a long time) or a contemporary figure or character (that is, someone well known who is alive today) and put this person in a crazy place or wild context, like Beyoncé living on Mars or Gandhi in a zombie apocalypse.

Look through newspapers and tabloids for funny, interesting, disturbing, or outlandish articles.

If you combine disparate (that is, contrasting or different) things and they "fuse together in a very unsettling way," chances are you've found or are near an interesting idea!

● FIRST LINES

A novel's opening sentence is the doorway into its story. When those first words captivate you, you find yourself crossing the threshold, unable to turn back, needing to know what's going to happen next.

Because they pack a punch, first lines are fun to read. So much fun that, according to *Uglies* author Scott Westerfeld, writers like "to geek out on first lines. We get all excited about collecting and trading them, having top-ten lists and all-time faves." So head to the library or your bookshelf, grab some novels, and start your own collection of favorite first lines.

Here are 10 of our all-time-fave opening lines:

"Where's Papa going with that ax?" said Fern to her mother as they were setting the table for breakfast. —*Charlotte's Web* by E. B. White

I had the story, bit by bit, from various people, and, as generally happens in such cases, each time it was a different story.
—*Ethan Frome* by Edith Wharton

It was a bright cold day in April, and the
clocks were striking thirteen.   —*1984*
                                by George Orwell

You better not never tell nobody but God.
                —*The Color Purple* by Alice Walker

Check this out. This dude named Andrew
Dahl holds the world record for blowing
up the most balloons . . . with his nose.
Yeah.   —*Ghost* by Jason Reynolds

My dad died twice. Once when he was
thirty-nine, and again four years later
when he was twelve.   —*Time Traveling*
                                with a Hamster
                                by Ross Welford

The night breathed through the apartment
like a dark animal.   —*Reckless*
                                by Cornelia Funke

I had just come to accept that my life would
be ordinary when extraordinary things
began to happen.   —*Miss Peregrine's Home*
                                for Peculiar Children
                                by Ransom Riggs

How does one describe Artemis Fowl?
Various psychiatrists have tried and
failed.   —*Artemis Fowl* by Eoin Colfer

My big brother reaches home in the dark
hours before dawn, when even ghosts take
their rest.   —*An Ember in the Ashes*
                           by Sabaa Tahir

You can add to your collection by writing a
bunch of vastly different first lines, too. This is a
great way to generate new story ideas. Give it a
shot by coming up with 5–10 funny, wacky, intriguing, sad, scary, or even nonsensical first lines.

DARE ⚡ MACHINE

Before you set out on your writing adventure, declare your writing challenge! Are you going to write a novel? A short story? An epic poem? A play? Something else entirely? Whatever writing project you're going to tackle, declare it now by shouting it out loud for all the world (or whoever is in close proximity) to hear.

"Hey, world, guess what? I'm going to write a _____!"

If you think it will help motivate you, you can also share your challenge on social media. Some people find that sharing their commitments with people near and far helps hold them accountable, while others find it stressful to have *everyone* know their intentions. Think about what you're comfortable with and the types of encouragement and support you'd like, and then go from there.

SET YOURSELF UP FOR SUCCESS THE NANOWRIMO WAY

Some people spend their lives dreaming about writing. Other people sit down and write.

Sure, the idea of *just doing it* is simple: all you have to do is walk to your desk, put your butt on the chair, and write. But in reality, doing this more than every once in a while, let alone making it through multiple stories (or other writing projects), is anything but easy.

If you want to go beyond *thinking* about writing and actually *be* a writer (that is, a person who practices writing, for many, many hours), you need to set yourself up for success. You need to make sure the things and people around you won't get in the way of reaching your goals.

For example, if you try to fly a kite in the rain,

you'll likely end up with a wet kite on the ground. To be successful, you could check the weather forecast and then plan to go out on a windy day. You're setting yourself up for success by taking the time to look ahead for the right conditions to fly a kite.

Here's another, more relevant example: If you tell yourself that you're going to write an entire novel on the day your aunt is getting married, when your whole family is expecting you to be not only available but also helpful and cheerful, you're likely *not* going to be successful. On the other hand, if you commit to writing a 10,000-word novel over the course of a month, you're giving yourself an achievable goal in an ample amount of time— you're setting yourself up for success! Go ahead and eat a stale piece of wedding cake to celebrate.

As you're reading this section, keep in mind that it will help you succeed on *every* writing project you tackle, no matter the length, no matter the genre. In fact, it's a good idea to revisit this section before you begin *any* new project, and also if you ever find yourself in a writing slump (that is, not writing for days on end).

Give Yourself a Deadline and a Goal

Having an idea is helpful, but really, you can start a story (or any writing project) with nothing more than a pen and a notebook (or a computer or a phone or even a roll of toilet paper and a pencil). *Completing* your writing project, however, isn't as easy. To reach "The End," you need two very special ingredients that are often left out of writing recipes.

You need a *deadline* and a *goal*. When combined, these two forces make a powerful concoction that fuels stories and keeps you trekking across your imaginary terrain until you reach your final destination.

● THE MIGHTY DEADLINE

Imagine if your teacher said, "Your homework is due whenever you want! Tomorrow, in a week, sometime before you graduate from high school, whenever!" You'd probably think you have the coolest teacher ever, right? But what are the chances you'd actually do your homework before your hair turns as gray as your teacher's? Pretty slim.

Without a firm deadline, this homework assignment becomes the very last thing on your to-do list—why do it now when you can do it later . . . or never? And sure, it's easy to put off things you don't feel like doing, like homework, regardless of their deadlines, but surprisingly, it's just as easy to put off things you love doing, like writing. So to make your writing project your top priority, you need a good, solid deadline.

Deadlines help us manage our time and give us a sense of urgency. When our phone buzzes and we dive thumbs-first into a texting frenzy, our deadline screams, "Noooo! Your friends can wait! You have to write *right now* because you have a deadline!" Or when the television magically turns on and we catch a glimpse of our favorite show, our deadline screams, "You don't have time for TV! You have to write *right now* because you have a deadline!"

Temptations beware: the deadline is a mighty force.

....

So how do you decide on a deadline?

NaNoWriMo's programs ask people to commit to their writing for, and complete their writing projects within, 30 days. Why 30 days and not, say, a year? Because getting to "The End" in 30 days feels achievable, while writing *every day for an entire year* feels daunting. And because when you only have 30 days to complete a writing project, you know that you can't spend 29 days on the opening line. Having a limited number of days forces you to manage your time and focus on forward progress.

When it comes to figuring out what your deadline should be, we've found that a month is a good amount of time to draft a novel (or a collection of short stories, a memoir, a play, or any other big writing project), but you should give yourself whatever amount of time feels right for you and your work. You want to have enough time to delve into your piece, but not so much time that you can't keep up the momentum.

Also, don't forget to build in some time to plan your story before you begin. For some, a week offers just the right amount of daydreaming, while for others, a month works better because it allows for some intense outlining. Keep in mind that prewriting is a lot like writing: you want to allot enough time to at least breathe life into a protagonist and figure out the basics of your plot, but not so much time that you plan your characters' every move.

collection of short stories

PLANNING 2 WEEKS
(March 18-31)

DEADLINE 1 MONTH
(April 1-30)

DARE ⚡ MACHINE

....

Activate Your Deadline

To activate your deadline and unleash its impene-
trable forces, grab your calendar and add your
start and end dates. So if you're going to write for
the month of November, for example, write "Start
writing!" on the first of November and "Deadline!"
on the thirtieth. (We recommend using permanent
marker.)

If your heart begins to race after completing
this task, your deadline is doing its job.

● A CHALLENGING BUT ACHIEVABLE GOAL

A deadline is great, but in order for it to really work its magic, it needs its partner: a goal.

If you're thinking, "Well, this is obvious—the goal is to write a story," you'd be correct, but there's a more specific goal you need, too. "Write a story" is a hard goal to visualize, or picture in your mind. Tangible goals (that is, clear goals that you can break down into smaller goals) are better motivators, which is why we recommend setting a particular number of words as a goal. That's right: in addition to finishing your story, you should try to write a specific number of words before your deadline. This type of goal is called a *word-count goal*. Word-count goals push people to get started, write more, and write faster (at least if a deadline is involved).

Here's something else about word-count goals: lots of successful authors use them, including Holly Black, Kate DiCamillo, and Stephen King:

I try to write a thousand words every day.
I've actually put up my daily word counts
online for my last several novels. I do this
to keep myself honest, saying exactly
when I wrote what part of the book.

—Holly Black,
author of the Spiderwick Chronicles

Two pages a day are what I ask of myself.
I never want to write, but I'm always glad
that I have done it.   —Kate DiCamillo,
author of *The Tale of Despereaux*

I like to get 10 pages a day, which amounts
to 2,000 words.   —Stephen King,
author of *It*

During National Novel Writing Month, adult writers set out to write a draft of a 50,000-word novel in the 30 days of November. Why is their goal 50,000 words? Because reaching this word count is challenging but achievable. Writing that many words in one month requires dedication, stamina, and often lots and lots of snacks. If you're trying to picture what 50,000 words looks like, here are a few books that are right about that length: *Speak* by Laurie Halse Anderson, *The Great Gatsby* by F. Scott Fitzgerald, and *The Giver* by Lois Lowry.

But you aren't an adult quite yet. And you shouldn't feel like your goal needs to be 50,000 words. For the Young Writers Program, students in grades K–12 pick their own challenging but do-able word-count goals. Some go for 1,000 words, while others shoot for 30,000 or more. Whether you choose a high word-count goal or a low one doesn't matter; what *does* matter is that you set a goal and push yourself toward it day after day after day until you reach it. Think of your word-count goal as the song in your playlist that pumps you up and keeps you going when your energy slows down.

DARE ⚡ MACHINE

Set Your Daily Word-Count Goal

 Set a timer for 20 minutes.

 Write at a comfortable pace for the entire 20 minutes. (Don't try to write or type as fast as you can.) You can write about anything you'd like, or use one of the following prompts:

* You're sitting on a park bench, reading a book, when a stranger sits down next to you and starts to cry. You hand her a tissue, and she begins to tell you a very odd story. . . .

* The person you have a crush on passes you a note during class. What does it say? How do you react?

* You're stuck in an elevator (for hours) with a celebrity.

* What's one thing you'd like to change in your school?

 When the time is up, check your word count. This number is your daily word-count goal (the number of words you'll need to write per day).

Depending on the type of project you'll be working on, your deadline, and how much time you'd like to dedicate to writing each day, you might want to adjust this goal. For example, if you want to write a short story in two weeks and you think you'll only have about 10–15 minutes a day to write, you'll likely do better with a lower daily word-count goal than the number you just came up with. Or if you're going to write a novel, your schedule is wide open, and there's nothing you'd rather do than write, write, write, give yourself a higher goal.

Figure Out Your Total Word-Count Goal

Here's how to get your total word-count goal: take your daily word-count goal and multiply it by the number of days you're going to write. For example, if your daily word-count goal is 300 words and you're going to write for 30 days, your total word-count goal will be 9,000 words.

Let's take a look at another example. If your daily word-count goal is 500 words and you're going to write for 5 days, multiply 500 by 5, and you'll get 2,500, which is your total word-count goal.

Now it's your turn. Follow this equation to figure out your total word-count goal:

Daily Word-Count Goal
x Total Number of Days
= Total Word-Count Goal

As you consider your own word-count goal, take a look at what these past NaNoWriMo participants have to say about setting yourself up for success:

Set your word-count goal to something a bit longer than any story you've ever written before, but don't overreach. I once tried to write a 20,000-word book when the biggest book I had ever written was 8,000 words. As you can imagine, that didn't end well. Remember, you can always change your word-count goal halfway through your story.

—Simon, age 11

Don't stress about what everyone else's word-count goals are! If you don't have time to write 30,000 words, don't make that your goal just because your friend is writing that much. If you have to limit yourself to 10,000 or even 2,500 because your life is just too busy to balance writing on top, don't think for a second that you're less of a writer for doing so. Write 10 words. Write 10 words right now. Boom, you're a writer.

—Robin, age 16

⊕ MEET YOUR INNER EDITOR (AND HOW QUANTITY LEADS TO QUALITY)

If your project still feels daunting even after nailing down a deadline and a goal, don't worry, you're not alone. Your Inner Editor might be making things more difficult than they need to be.

"Inner what?" you might be thinking. "You must be mistaken. I don't have an Inner Editor."

Ah, but you do! We all have one, even the most famous writers out there. It's that gnarly (and impeccably dressed) beast who hovers over your work, pointing out typos and misspellings and every awkward sentence on the page.  Sometimes, when it's feeling particularly nasty, your Inner Editor will sidle up real close and whisper in your ear, "Wow, you're a *really* terrible writer! How 'bout you call it quits already?"

Sound familiar? When your Inner Editor is bossing

you around, it's easy to get stuck writing and re-writing the same sentence or paragraph over and over again. And because your Inner Editor is a nosy creature, it can show up even when you're *not* writing: You may have heard its irreverent voice trying to convince you not to try out for the school play because, in its words, "you will definitely trip onstage and embarrass yourself and everyone in the entire school will laugh at you." Or maybe you've felt butterflies in your stomach before a big soccer game. Guess what? Those butterflies aren't actually butterflies; they're your Inner Editor throwing a monster-size tantrum, banging its fists against your insides, making you feel extra nervous and queasy.

The fact of the matter is, your Inner Editor is powerful—and perfection is enticing. If you're not careful, it can stop you from writing entirely. It can hold you in a headlock, give you a noogie, and prevent you from braving the page, telling your story, and sharing your truth.

But fortunately, you have access to your Inner Editor's kryptonite: a deadline and a goal. Having to complete a set number of words over a set number of days forces you to keep writing and stops you from deleting sentences or scenes that you're not entirely happy with. When you have a word-count goal and a deadline, you end up working for your Inner Editor's nemesis: *quantity* (a particular number of words). (In Part 3, you'll learn more about your wily Inner Editor before officially saying farewell to it.)

"Wait, whaaaaat?!" you might say. "The Inner Editor stuff makes sense and all, but isn't *quality* the only thing that really matters when it comes to writing? This *quantity* stuff sounds fishy!"

Yeah, we know it sounds a bit wacky to suggest that the number of words you write matters more, at first, than whether the words make sense when they're strung together across an entire story, but hear us out.

Writing for Quantity Leads to Quality Writing

Many writers who write for *quality first* get stuck writing and rewriting the same sentence, paragraph, or chapter over and over again (sometimes for years!) before dumping their great idea into a drawer (or trash can), never to be seen again. Take it from *Crewel* author Gennifer Albin, who has experienced this firsthand: "I'd always wanted to write a book, but every time I tried I abandoned it a few chapters in. My husband started to tease me that my obituary would read 'author of the twenty most promising first chapters ever written.'"

Focusing on *quantity* first, however, will help you reach the end of your story by your deadline. You'll find yourself writing faster than you've ever written before. You'll find yourself (repeatedly) checking the number of words you've written. You'll find that you're pushing yourself to write more and more and more.

Will your first draft be riddled with grammatical errors and shaky plotlines? Probably. But guess what? Every author begins with a messy rough draft—it's a critical part of the creative process! All types of creators, from authors to sculptors to architects, work through lots and lots (and lots) of ideas until they find a version that works. (The fancy name for this is *creative ideation*.)

Remember the inventor Thomas Edison? He worked through many (failed) experiments before he came up with the practical electric lightbulb. Just think, if he had given up after his first botched attempt, you might be reading this by candlelight. Edison learned from his mistakes, and so can we, as writers and as humans.

Being a writer is actually a lot like being an inventor. Like most inventions, your characters, settings, and plot probably won't work perfectly from the get-go—you'll have to experiment and be okay with imperfection, because eventually your story's gears will begin to turn, the lights will go on, and everything will fall into place. None of this can happen, however, without a whole lot of writing—that is, *quantity*.

Once you've reached your word-count goal, you can begin to steer toward *quality*. (That is, you can revise and edit.) As author Jodi Picoult said, "You can always edit a bad page, but you can't edit a blank page." And fortunately, you know a little someone who's very astute and would love nothing more than to help make your work the best it can be. When you're ready, just give your Inner Editor a yell and it'll come bounding home.

So to wrap up: A deadline and a goal will help keep your Inner Editor quiet, which will help you finish a draft of your writing project. Mistakes, even messy ones, help us grow.

DETERMINE WHAT TYPE OF WRITER YOU ARE

Are you a *planner*, a *pantser*, or a *plantser*? These funny names are what we use to describe different types of writers. Identifying your type will help you manage your prewriting and writing time better, and it's fun to join forces and commiserate with other writers who share your planning, or lack of planning, tendencies.

Planners like to approach the blank page with a map (or outline) in hand. They make character sketches and outlines and plot diagrams and intricate maps showing every nook and cranny of their fictional landscapes. They arrive at the blank page knowing exactly where they're headed.

Pantsers fly by the seat of their pants, making their way through their stories without any plan at all (and sometimes without even an inkling of an idea). When they get to the blank page, they say, "All right, let's find out where we're going!"

Plantsers fall somewhere in the middle. They have a loose plan to serve as a guide, but they're also drawn toward spontaneity, so they're open to meandering away from their original ideas. They begin writing with some knowledge of their destination, but without a definite route to get there.

One type of writer isn't better—or more successful—than another, but it's still helpful to consider which type you identify with most. If you feel more comfortable with a concrete plan, you'll know you need plenty of time to get one in order before beginning a project. Or if you know that making an outline isn't helpful to you, you can get yourself ready to dive into your story.

Need help figuring out which type of writer you are? Take this short quiz to find out. (Don't worry, it's not graded.)

For each prompt, select the answer that you most relate to:

I make plans for the weekend . . .

    a. At least a week before, if not weeks in advance.

    b. On the Thursday or Friday before the weekend.

    c. Never. When I wake up on Saturday, I eat breakfast and take it from there.

I write down my school assignments . . .

    a. In my homework planner, and I include all of the important guidelines and parameters.

    b. In my homework planner (or on a sticky note, scrap of paper, or the back of my hand), with very few details.

    c. Nowhere. Why would I write my homework down when I have such an awesome memory?

I decide what I'm going to wear to school . . .

    a. The night before (and, TBH, sometimes even a few days before). And I always lay out my clothes to make the morning easy.

    b. When I wake up in the morning. I give myself a little extra time to get dressed.

    c. By grabbing whatever I can find that morning.

Before I write an essay or research paper, I . . .

a. Spend a good amount of time organizing my notes and creating a detailed outline.

b. Pull together a quick outline to help myself get organized.

c. Don't do anything. I use my notes and do additional research as I write.

For my birthday, I . . .

a. Plan a party. I even use a spreadsheet to organize all of the details.

b. Invite a few friends over for a sleepover. I usually text them to see if they're free a few days before my birthday.

c. Love surprise parties! The thrill of not knowing what's going to happen on my birthday is the best. (And if no one plans a surprise party for me, I know I'll come up with an idea to make the day special, because I love spontaneity.)

Count the number of *a*s, *b*s, and *c*s that you chose.

a____ b____ c____

Whatever type of writer you are today might be different from the type of writer you are in a week or a month or a year. Take *Divergent* author Veronica Roth, for instance. She goes back and forth between types. In a NaNoWriMo pep talk, she said, "It is not important that you stay the same writer you are now, or that you have a definite routine or pattern. I started my first book in the middle, with no outline, and finished my third book with a detailed one, written from beginning to end. I thought I knew what kind of writer I was, but ultimately I found those definitions limiting rather than freeing. If I can let them go, I can become whatever writer each story requires me to be."

Lots of writers start out as planners, but when they try pantsing it, they're surprised to find that this method suits them better. And vice versa: sometimes pantsers will give outlines a whirl and never go back to their wild and crazy seat-of-their-pants days. Ultimately, you make your own rules, and those rules can change whenever you want.

If you're curious about why some people are drawn to one type over another, take a look at the pros and cons of each:

Pros of Planning

 It gives you a sense of direction.

 You can write with the ending in mind.

 There's a smaller chance your story will
go wildly astray.

 You can work through character, setting,
and plot issues before you begin.

Cons of Planning

 Outlining can sometimes hinder your
characters' journeys. They might not want to
go where your outline tells them to go, which
can create a giant wall between them and the
rest of your story.

 It can become an excuse not to write.

 Following an outline can feel like you're
following a recipe, which can restrict your
imagination.

Wonder which authors are Team Planner? Here are a few planners discussing their reasons for choosing this method:

Monster author Walter Dean Myers was a planner. According to him, "planning a book does not limit your creativity." He used planning as a way to explore his book ideas. "Is there only enough material for a short story? Is my idea clear enough to work toward a logical conclusion?" Even though he started with a plan, he also created space for flexibility. "I plan books scene by scene, and give myself permission to change anything if I come up with a better idea." The plans that work best are flexible, especially for the first draft, because you're exploring your story and you don't know where the paths will take you.

R. L. Stine, author of the Goosebumps series, also falls into the planner camp. "No one likes to outline—but I can't work without one. I think that's one reason I'm so prolific—I take a week and I plan everything. I do all the thinking beforehand."

Pros of Pantsing or Plantsing

 It gives your characters and their journeys more freedom to change and develop along the way.

 Your imagination will spontaneously lead you to places you didn't think you were capable of creating.

 You'll take more creative risks because your novel isn't contained by any boundaries.

 You can begin your story right away instead of spending time on an outline.

Cons of Pantsing or Plantsing

 You don't have a sense of who your characters are from the start or of where your story is going to go.

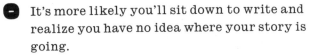 Without having put time into making a plan, it can sometimes feel easier to give up on a story.

It's more likely you'll sit down to write and realize you have no idea where your story is going.

Team Pantser and Team Plantser also boast notable authors. Read about their processes and reasons for choosing these methods:

Author Erin Morgenstern, who wrote the first draft of her novel *The Night Circus* during NaNoWriMo, is a pantser. "*The Night Circus* began as an unplanned tangent in the middle of a different NaNo project. I got bored and sent my characters to a circus. The circus was much more interesting than anything else that was happening." Her flexibility and spontaneity led her to an entirely new story, one that worked so well it became a bestselling novel (after many rounds of revision and edits, of course).

George R. R. Martin, author of *A Game of Thrones*, hates outlines. As for his process, he says, "I have a broad sense of where the story is going; I know the end, I know the end of the principal characters, and I know the major turning points and events from the books, the climaxes for each book, but I don't necessarily know each twist and turn along the way. That's something I discover in the course of writing and that's what makes writing enjoyable. I think if I outlined comprehensively and stuck to the outline, the actual writing would be boring."

Diana Wynne Jones, author of *Howl's Moving Castle*, was more of a plantser than a pantser—she did a bit of planning before she started her stories, but not a whole lot. She said, "When I start writing a book, I know the beginning and what probably happens in the end, plus a tiny but extremely bright picture of something going on in the middle. Often this tiny picture is so different from the beginning that I get really excited trying to think how they got from the start to there. This is the way to get a story moving, because I can't wait to find out. And by not planning it any more than that I leave space for the story to go in unexpected ways."

Another writer who's a plantser is *Once and for All* author Sarah Dessen. "I don't outline, because I don't want to have to follow a plan. But I do need *some* sense of direction, so I use what I call my skeleton. It's my first scene, climactic scene, last scene, and first line. I don't start until I have them in place. Often they will change over the course of a first draft, but it gets me there."

We advise trying each method at some point—flying by the seat of your pants and planning ahead of time—so that you can decide which works better for you.

START A WRITING
ROUTINE

What do Oprah Winfrey (talk show host), Barack Obama (forty-fourth president of the United States), and Kurt Vonnegut (*Slaughterhouse-Five* author) have in common? (This sounds like the beginning of a joke, but, alas, it's not—you could, however, turn it into one if you'd like.) All of these people have (or had, in the case of Vonnegut) particular routines they follow every day:

Winfrey meditates every morning for 20 minutes (and sometimes at night, too); Obama starts his day with exercise; and Vonnegut wrote early in the morning for 90 minutes, gave himself a break for breakfast at 8:00 a.m., and then continued writing until 10:00 a.m.

Sticking to a routine isn't unique to these three people. In fact, many successful people, in every profession, incorporate routines into their days. In terms of writing, having a routine gets rid of that "how am I ever going to squeeze writing into my hectic day?" feeling because you know exactly when you're going to get to your story: depending on your routine, you might write for 20 minutes before breakfast or 30 minutes before bed, or both! Following a routine creates predictability and consistency, and helps you prioritize the things that are important to you.

Get started on creating a writing routine that'll stick:

Determine the time of day you write best.

Not sure how to figure this out? Try writing for 20 minutes in the morning, which might mean waking up 20 minutes earlier than you normally do; 20 minutes at midday, maybe at lunch or recess or during a really boring class; and 20 minutes in the evening, perhaps after dinner or right before you go to bed. Once you've experimented with how your imagination functions throughout the day, decide when your writing routine will take place.

Give yourself a time limit. Yes, you have a daily word-count goal, but giving yourself a set amount of time each day will force you to get started right away. Be reasonable with the amount of time you give yourself: if you say you're going to write for two hours every morning before school, you might find your routine starting to fizzle by day three. Start with 20–60 minutes a day, and increase from there if it feels right. Know that you might have to play around with your regular schedule to make space for your writing routine. And if you're having trouble finding time in your day, think about what an ancient Chinese philosopher once said: "Time is a created thing. To say 'I don't have time' is like saying 'I don't want to.'"

Create a ritual to mark the beginning of your writing time and to celebrate the end of it. Maybe your ritual begins with putting your phone out of reach and ends with a treat, like a piece of your favorite candy or a special snack that's reserved for your post-writing reward. Or maybe you start your ritual by listening to your favorite song to get you in the writing mood and end it by doing jumping jacks while yelling at the top of your lungs. Having a ritual will help you transition into and out of the writing zone—and more important, rituals are fun!

Like your novel, the "first draft" of your routine might not work perfectly. But that's okay, because like your novel, you can revise your routine as many times as you'd like until it feels right to you.

Before you continue on, let's take a minute to huddle up and review what you read in Part 1:

>> Story ideas are all around you. To catch one or more, you can try mining your life, making lists, looking for opposites or wildly differing elements, and reading the first lines of books.

>> When you set yourself up for success, your imagination has the freedom to go wild on the page.

>> Some ways to set yourself up for success are activating a deadline, setting a word-count goal, writing a first draft for quantity, thinking about the type of writer you are (or would like to be), and creating a writing routine.

Now, onward! In Part 2, you'll set out on a series of quests to learn important craft techniques, and you'll begin to plan your own story.

② GET SET

Grab a satchel or a suitcase or a giant, compostable bag, and collect an assortment of valuable items to aid your imagination in creating worlds and people and elves and enchanted forests and realistic depictions of your protagonist's best friend storming off after a life-altering fight over who wore it best. In Part 2, you'll navigate through the prewriting stage of the writing process by completing a series of quests that will help bring your story to life.

THE QUEST FOR YOUR STORY'S PLAN

Say the word "quest" out loud. It is an
extraordinary word, isn't it? So small and
yet so full of wonder, so full of hope.
—Kate DiCamillo, *The Tale of Despereaux*

You've named your adventure, triggered your
deadline, and set your goal—in other words, you've
gotten everything *outside* of your story ready for
success. But what about the *inside* of your novel?
There are some things to consider before you head
out on your grand writing adventure, like, who's
going to be the hero (aka the protagonist)? What
are your characters' motivations? What are their
biggest fears? What do they see when they look out
their windows? Are they in the same place at the
end of the story—or are they now on a different
planet, or in a different galaxy?

In Part 2, you'll throw your writing armor on and complete a series of quests that will give you critical information about the craft of writing and also help you to plan your story.

During these quests, you'll decide on your genre and whether your protagonist comes face-to-face with flying sharks, futuristic fire-breathing robots, or the school's steely-eyed principal—or all of the above! As the writer of your story, you'll get to create your characters, determine what they want most, and craft the world in which they live.

Pantsers, we suggest you read through the quests, too, even though you're not planning on using an outline. Learning about the craft of writing, like what makes a character go from boring to interesting and how to convey mood through setting, will make you a stronger writer.

Here's a brief rundown of the quests you'll be facing:

QUEST 1: Meet your mentor. To get started, you'll grab your favorite book and tear into it to learn craft techniques from its author.

QUEST 2: Recruit your characters. In this quest, you'll develop complex new beings, including your story's hero (the protagonist).

QUEST 3: Plot your plot. During this quest, you'll pave the road for your characters to follow, from the beginning of your story to the end.

QUEST 4: Build your story's world. In this quest, you'll make mountains and buildings and houses and thunderstorms and sun rays using nothing more than the power of your imagination. You'll give your characters ground to walk on, beds to sleep in, and jackets for inclement weather.

After you've made it through each quest, you'll be ready to cross the threshold from your ordinary, everyday life into the extraordinary world of your story; you'll be ready to brave the page.

NOTE: There isn't one right way to complete this part of the book; you can begin with the first quest or start with the third. We put the quests in an order that makes sense to us, but that doesn't mean it's the right order for you. When you're done, you might have a mile-long road map marking every twist and turn of your story, or you might end up with nothing more than the name of your protagonist and the town they live in. The only way to *not* make it through the quests is to skip this section entirely.

One last thing (*takes your face in our hands and looks you in the eye*): You are mighty and brave, and you will use the magic of your imagination to create something out of nothing. You are a writer.

QUEST 1:
MEET YOUR MENTOR

I can remember the novels and stories that
seemed to me revelations: wells of beauty
and pleasure that were also textbooks,
private lessons in the art of fiction.
—Francine Prose, *Reading Like a Writer*

A Look Inside Your Favorite Book

Here's a fact you might not have learned in school:
in addition to writing a whole lot, authors also
read a whole lot.

They read for the same reasons non-writers
read—to learn, to communicate, to be entertained—
but readers who are also writers read for another

reason: to learn how books work. Sure, it seems obvious: stories have a beginning, a middle, and an end. While that's true, some books have beginnings that sweep us away, while others have beginnings that make us cry hot tears of boredom. And some books have characters that we remember long after we close the book, while others have characters who disintegrate into thin air even before we reach "The End."

So what makes us love one book and despise another? What did the author of your favorite book do differently from the author of your least favorite book?

Just like a botanist dissects plants to learn about their various parts and how they work, your job as a writer is to dissect your favorite book to see its inner workings—what did the author do to make the characters compelling, the setting vivid, the plot interesting?

Beneath their surface, books hold a wealth of information: if you take the time to look closely, you'll see which elements you're drawn to, and then you can include those in your own writing. Books also serve as fantastic mentors—and they're always available, 24-7, so if you happen to be working on your story in the middle of the night and you can't figure out how to transition from one chapter to the next, grab your favorite book and check out what the author did to move the reader onward. (You should never copy from books, but you can—and should!—use them for ideas and to learn techniques.)

DARE ⚡ MACHINE

Creepy settings! Weird but relatable characters! Funny dialogue! Your favorite book is riddled with all sorts of treasures. So roll up your sleeves, grab that book, and head out on a scavenger hunt to uncover the gems that lie between the front and back covers.

Here's a list of things to seek out in your favorite book. Collect them all and you win . . . a better understanding of how great books are constructed! Wahoo! Now go get 'em.

1 List the main characters, and then describe each of them in three words.

2 Write down which character is the most important. Explain how you know they're the most important.

3 Pick your favorite scene and draw a picture of it. (Notice the words the author uses to help paint that picture in your mind.)

4 Determine who's telling the story (for example, the main character, a narrator, an unknown character). You'll learn more about perspective and point of view in Quest 2.

Describe how the story begins. What pulls you, the reader, into the story?

 Write down where and when the story takes place.

 Write a haiku about what the main character wants more than anything in the world. (Or if you're not in a poetic mood, just write down what the character desires.)

 List the obstacles in their way.

 Describe how the story ends.

How'd you do? Pat yourself on the back if you found all the items on the scavenger hunt list. Be sure to hold on to these answers (and your favorite book), so that you can refer to them for ideas, advice, and inspiration when you're working on your own story.

QUEST 2:
RECRUIT YOUR
CHARACTERS

It begins with a character, usually, and once
he stands up on his feet and begins to move,
all I do is trot along behind him with a paper
and pencil trying to keep up long enough to
put down what he says and does.

—William Faulkner

Roll Call

Think back to Quest 1. What do you remember
most about your favorite book? Chances are, you
remember the characters. You might even remember them as you do a friend or family member. Like
the world we live in, stories typically have a whole
cast of characters, each of whom falls into one of
the following categories: *protagonist*, *supporting
character*, and *antagonist*.

● CHARACTER CAST LIST

Protagonist: The character who plays the starring role. We get to know this complex character well throughout the book. (Some famous protagonists include Harry Potter, Katniss Everdeen, and Cinderella.)

Supporting Characters: The characters who tend to help or be close to the protagonist (for example, Ron Weasley and Hermione Granger in the Harry Potter series). Some supporting characters show up often in a story (like Ron and Hermione), while others pop in less frequently (like Neville Longbottom). These types of characters also have varying degrees of importance. Some roles these characters might play: the protagonist's parents, friends, teachers, and neighbors.

Antagonist: The character (or force) that gets in the protagonist's way. Some antagonists are evil, and some are just jealous, obnoxious, mean, or a combination of all of these traits. Other antagonists aren't physical beings at all—these are called *abstract antagonists*. Some examples of abstract antagonists are nature (the Canadian wilderness in *Hatchet*), illness (rabies in *Old Yeller*), and a corrupt government (the Empire in *An Ember in the Ashes*). Character or abstract, the antagonist tries to stop the protagonist from getting what they want (whether it's Cinderella's stepmother making her clean the house instead of going to the ball, or the Party's inescapable surveillance of its citizens making it difficult and frightening for Winston Smith to think for himself in *1984*).

Even though the protagonist has the leading role, every character that lives in a story is important. Each person (or animal, beast, alien) who walks across your page will be an individual with their own hairstyle, taste in music, and deep, dark secrets.

In order for the characters to be more than just names on a page, you, the author, need to know each character well. But don't worry, you don't need to know everything about everyone before you begin: when you unleash your motley crew of characters onto the page, they'll steer you in new directions and reveal more to you about who they are as people. To get started, all you really need is your protagonist, the thing they want most, and an idea of what might get in their way.

DARE ⚡ MACHINE

Who are your characters? And how can you get to know them? One fun way to begin is to create a pretend social media page for each of your characters, including the protagonist, antagonist, and as many supporting characters as you'd like.

Keep these profiles in a notebook or in a document and make sure to have them handy, since you'll want to refer to them throughout the writing process. Also, leave some room on each profile or skip pages so that you can continue to add notes about each character. (Even though you're taking inspiration from real life, remember that your characters are fictional: don't base them on—or use the names of—your friends or enemies.)

For each profile, include:

 The character's name and age

 Role (protagonist, antagonist, supporting character)

 A drawing of the character (or a description of what they look like)

 Where they live

- ❯❯ Favorite activities, books, music, food

- ❯❯ Pet peeves

- ❯❯ Family members

- ❯❯ Three words that describe them

- ❯❯ Three things they like to post about on their social media page

---

🌐 https://yourcharacters/Selena ☆

 yourCharacters

Selena Moonstone

♡ 🖼 📹 👍 ⑦ ⓘ

ABOUT ME:
· Age 14

HOBBIES:
· Reading books
· Casting spells
· Befriending cats

SELENA POSTED:

I learned a new spell today!

📣 Antagonist dislikes this

SELENA POSTED:

DARE ⚡ MACHINE

Is your protagonist open-minded and hardworking? A natural leader and sensitive? Curious and unpredictable? How do the protagonist's and your other characters' traits affect their friendships and the way they interact with the world? Give them a personality test to find out! (Tell your characters not to worry—some tests are more fun than others. Algebra test? Not so fun. Personality test? Super fun!)

Find a personality test (there are plenty online, including Myers–Briggs and 16Personalities) and explore your characters' personality types by answering questions for them.

Complex Characters

When we read books we love, the characters become our friends (and sometimes our enemies). We laugh when they do something funny, we cry when they get their hearts broken, and we miss them when we finish their story. We remember characters we love as real people, not as figments of an author's imagination.

These memorable characters are *complex*, just like living and breathing people. They have opinions and quirks and emotions and secrets.

Complex characters have depth: the better you get to know them, the more interesting they become. They also grow and change over time—by the end of the story, they aren't the same people they were in the beginning. Complex characters often have realizations or epiphanies (those sudden moments when the little lightbulb floating above your head turns on and you're like, "Oh, I totally get it!"), and they often learn something about themselves and the world they live in.

The opposite of a complex character is a *flat* one. To put it simply, flat characters are boring. Like an open can of soda left out for too long, they lack fizzle and pop. Flat characters might exhibit one or two traits that make them likable—or despicable—but they don't grow and change over time; at the end of a story, they're exactly who they were in the beginning.

Take a look at this character:

Skittle is a 15-year-old who has lots of friends. It's the beginning of the school year, and she's already on the Honors List. As Skittle makes her way through tenth grade, she continues to do well in her classes. And like the year before and the year before that, she's the most popular girl in the school. If given the choice, Skittle wouldn't change anything about her life!

This version of Skittle is *flat* because there's nothing incredible or unique about her and there isn't anything in particular that she wants. Also, she doesn't change at all over the course of the story. But just because she's a little boring now doesn't mean we need to scrap her and start over; instead, we can add layers to her character and her life. By adding a little more texture, a little more spice, we can transform Skittle from a two-dimensional flat character into a three-dimensional complex one.

Here's a version of Skittle as a more complex character:

Skittle hates her name. She's lived with it for 15 years, and she refuses to live with it for another day. Her parents named her after their favorite candy, something Skittle thinks they should be locked up for. To make matters worse, everyone at school—except for her best and only friend, Luna—makes fun of her eccentric, "sweet" name.

What Skittle doesn't know yet is that her parents lied to her about her name's origin. When she learns the truth, her entire outlook on life shifts: she no longer worries about things like her curly red hair being frizzy, or the fact that she's a foot taller than all the other girls at school. She doesn't even care when the boys in her grade snicker at her as she eats her Halloween candy. Now all she worries about is how to keep her parents' terrible secret.

In this version, Skittle isn't perfect, nor is her life. She's complex because she has wants and frustrations and challenges . . . and secrets.

DARE ⚡ MACHINE

Ernest Hemingway said, "When writing a novel a writer should create living people; people not characters. A *character* is a caricature." In other words, the characters in your novel should be complex, layered, and multidimensional, just as living people are.

Pick a real-life person you're close to, like a friend, family member, or teacher. Then make a list of their physical traits—describe what you see when you look at this person. Next, make a list of their personality traits—what kind of person are they? Think about what makes this person interesting or quirky or unique. Write down as much about this person as you can.

As you're developing your characters, keep in mind all the things that make living people fascinating and complex, and then incorporate those elements into the people who inhabit your story.

DARE ⚡ MACHINE

To make your characters more believable, grab an invisibility cloak and a notebook and take a little field trip to study people in their natural habitats. You could sit in a crowded restaurant, walk around a shopping mall, or go for a ride on a bus. Wherever you end up, make sure you're inconspicuous (that is, don't be obvious; be sly like a spy) and that you have your parents' permission to be there. (If you're not able to get out of the house, turn the TV on and find a show where people are talking to each other. A reality show or talk show would work well.)

In your notebook, jot down descriptions of the people around you. What do you see? What do you hear? Is someone slurping their soup or walking with a little skip in their step or scowling at the people around them? Do you see someone who's broad-shouldered and tall like a football player, or someone who's flowy and petite like a reed dancing in the wind?

Take note of mannerisms (*teenage girl nibbles on her nails as she reads her book*), style choices (*older man with a green spiky Mohawk is wearing a dark-blue business suit*), and anything else unique or interesting that catches your eye.

Observing people and the way they interact with the world around them will help you develop believable characters across all genres. Even if your characters are 100-foot-tall cats or pint-sized purple dragons, you'll want to incorporate human qualities into them or you'll end up with a very confusing story.

Here are a few fun exercises from authors you can do to help develop your characters:

Watch the news, eavesdrop on the people at Trader Joe's, go to all the parties. Your characters are out there, waiting to be discovered.   —Stacey Lee,
   award-winning author of *Outrun the Moon*

Write a long list of all your characters. Then, start drawing random lines connecting random characters to each other. Don't think—just connect. Afterward, look down at your page. Try to figure out a connection between each of the two random

characters you just linked—something
scandalous, maybe, or something sweet.
Something three-dimensional and
unexpected. Some explosive scene that
throws the two together.

—Marie Lu,
New York Times bestselling author
of the Legend trilogy

Whose Story Is This?

You know your protagonist and some of the supporting characters. You might have a good sense of your story's antagonist, too. But do you know who's going to *tell* your story? Will it be your protagonist? An unnamed narrator? One of the supporting characters? When you decide who's telling your story, you're deciding on your story's point of view (or POV, as we like to call it).

There are three main types of POV:

First Person: The narrator, who could be the protagonist or a different character who's acting as an observer, tells the story from their perspective, using the pronouns *I*, *me*, and *my*. *Simon vs. the Homo Sapiens Agenda* by Becky Albertalli, is an example of a book told in the first person: "I squeeze through my row and back down the stairs, feeling like every eye in the stadium is on me."

> ⊕ **Pros:** Readers get to know the narrator really well. It puts them right into that character's shoes, allowing them to think, see, and feel what that character is thinking, seeing, and feeling.

Cons: Readers only get the narrator's perspective, which means they only get insight into what that character knows or experiences.

Second Person: The narrator tells the story directly to another character (often the protagonist), using the pronoun *you*. It can feel like the story is being told from your perspective, making you, the reader, a character in the book. Using the second person almost feels like writing a letter. *Bright Lights, Big City*, by Jay McInerney, is an example of a book told in the second person: "You are not the kind of guy who would be at a place like this at this time of the morning."

Pros: As the writer, you get to tell readers what to feel and how to react. Because the book is speaking directly to them, readers feel like they are in the story. This point of view also gives the reader a sense of control, as though they are the ones deciding what to do next.

Cons: When you write in this POV, you use the pronoun *you* a whole lot, which can get tiring—for you, the writer, and for the reader. In addition, people don't always like to be told what to do or how to feel; this perspective can push readers away instead of pulling them in.

Third Person: The narrator tells us the thoughts, feelings, and actions of one or more characters, using the pronouns *he*, *she*, and *they*. *Number the Stars*, by Lois Lowry, is an example of a book told in the third person: "Annemarie adjusted the thick leather pack on her back so that her schoolbooks balanced evenly. 'Ready?' She looked at her best friend."

⊕ Pros: Even though there is still one protagonist that readers get to know best, they are able to learn what several different characters are doing and how they're feeling. You can also give readers information that the characters aren't aware of—and give characters information that isn't shared with readers.

⊖ Cons: Because there is more distance between the reader and the protagonist, readers might not feel as connected to the character. In addition, if you try to capture too many characters' thoughts, feelings, and actions, you might cause your readers to lose focus.

Picking your story's POV can be tricky, but know that, like everything else, you can change it later—you can even change it halfway through if you think a different perspective would be better! (But only in the first draft: unless done intentionally and carefully, changing point of view midway through a book can be confusing for readers.)

DARE ⚡ MACHINE

Using the first-person POV, write a paragraph about a grizzly bear playing in a stream.

Now, write a paragraph about the same topic using the second-person POV.

Finally, write about the grizzly bear from the third-person POV.

What did you notice about the different perspectives? Which POV do you think worked best for this exercise?

But I Want It Now!

All stories—no matter their genre, whether they're rife with dragons and wizards or take place in a doctor's office—are, at their core, about the same thing: a character's journey to get what they want most in the world.

Don't believe it? Check out these examples:

The Wonderful Wizard of Oz: After
being whisked away by a powerful tornado, poor
Dorothy just wants to go home. To get back to
Kansas, she takes a long journey along the Yellow
Brick Road and meets some very interesting
friends (and foes).

Charlie and the Chocolate Factory:
Charlie Bucket wants chocolate—and a better life
for himself and his family. His yearning for a
sweeter existence leads him to some wacky
adventures at Willy Wonka's Chocolate Factory.

Where the Wild Things Are: Max puts
on his wolf costume, in search of fun and mischief,
which results in his being put to bed without any
dinner. Max wants to have fun, but the thing he
really yearns for is attention, a warm embrace,
and to be with his family.

The Giver: Jonas learns what he wants most
after becoming the Receiver of Memory, an
important job in the Community. After
witnessing something disturbing, Jonas knows
that he wants two things: to save baby Gabriel and
to try to change the Community by causing them
to experience emotion through his memories.

The House on Mango Street: As
Esperanza explores her neighborhood and the
world around her, we learn that her heart's desire
is a better life.

In each of these stories (and in most others that you know), the thing the protagonists want most is their *motive* (that is, their reason for doing something), and the *motive* puts each story into *motion*.

(Want to impress your English teacher? The Latin root *mot* means "move"—the protagonist's *motive* is the thing that *moves* them, or puts them in *motion*, to act.)

But a character's want or need on its own won't make for an interesting story. It's the obstacles in the character's way (that is, the internal and external conflicts) that really drive the story from the first sentence to the very last.

Internal conflict is a struggle inside a character's mind. The character wants something, but there's something that's holding them back, like a phobia, a secret, guilt, shame, or fear. (Internal conflict is sometimes referred to as *character vs. self*.)

>> In Laurie Halse Anderson's *Speak*, the protagonist, Melinda, wants to tell her friends what happened to her at an end-of-summer party, but the traumatic impact of the incident as well as her fears keep her silent (for a bit, at least).

On the outside, Liz Emerson in Amy Zhang's *Falling into Place* appears to have it all, but on the inside, she's full of self-doubt and struggles with depression.

 In Angie Thomas's *The Hate U Give*, Starr struggles with whether or not she should tell people she was there when her childhood best friend was killed by a police officer.

External conflict is a struggle between the character and an outside force (a physical or abstract antagonist). External conflicts typically fall into one of the following categories: character vs. character (Cinderella against her stepmother); character vs. society (Katniss against the corrupt Capitol in *The Hunger Games*); character vs. the natural world (Buck, the dog star in *The Call of the Wild*, against the unforgiving Alaskan land); and character vs. technology or the supernatural (Victor Frankenstein against Frankenstein's monster).

Stories that hook readers and keep them engaged have *both* types of conflict: internal and external (though not necessarily in equal amounts). Internal conflict helps readers understand and feel empathetic toward characters and their motives, and external conflict creates action.

Take a look at the following two examples:

A hungry boy walks to the market, buys a chocolate bar, and then eats it on his way home.

A boy walks to the corner store for a snack because he's terribly hungry (the cupboards in his house are empty), only to find he doesn't have any money in his wallet. He's too scared to ask if he could pay for a Snickers bar later because he's seen the woman at the counter scream at other customers before for not having the right amount of money. He sees that she's distracted by her phone, so he crouches down, pretends to tie his shoe, and stuffs the Snickers bar into his sock. His heart pounds and his palms sweat as he limps across the store with his pilfered loot. But then, right before he reaches the door, a police officer saunters in. The boy finds himself face-to-face with his future: he could still turn around and put the Snickers bar back on the shelf and continue being the good boy that he's always been, or he could try his luck and possibly forever alter the road ahead of him.

Which example shows conflict? Which story would you rather read, the first or the second?

In the first example, the boy is hungry, but there's nothing stopping him from getting the thing he wants (a chocolate bar). This story line makes for a terribly dull (and terribly short) read.

In the second example, the boy has the same desire (food), but there are obstacles in his way. The external obstacles are his empty wallet and a mean cashier, and the internal conflict, which takes place inside his mind, is that he knows he shouldn't steal. The story is interesting because we want to know how the character will overcome (or succumb to) the roadblocks in his way.

Once you've discovered what your characters want most in the world, it can feel particularly cruel to throw traps and barriers in their way, but rest assured that they will persevere and end up stronger than they were before!

DARE ⚡ MACHINE

A protagonist can have all sorts of desires: they might want a material item, like a family heirloom that went missing; or a particular feeling, like being loved; or to win something, like their school's spelling bee.

Make a list of 5–10 things your protagonist wants.

Next, circle the one they want more than anything in the world.

Finally, come up with five things that might stop your protagonist from getting what they want. Think about both external obstacles and internal beliefs or fears.

By exploring your protagonist's desires and struggles, you'll begin to uncover your story's plot.

QUEST 3:
PLOT YOUR PLOT

Things don't just happen. People make them
happen.   —Diana Wynne Jones,
                    author of *Howl's Moving Castle*

The Plot Equation

Stories take many different forms—some are
action-packed, others romantic, funny, or sad;
some are told in chronological order, others
through flashbacks—but ultimately, no matter
what they're about or how they're structured, most
stories' plots boil down to this: characters working through conflicts as they chase after their
dreams.

If plot were a math equation, it might look something like this:

characters
+ desires
+ conflict
= story

Now, because we're good mathematicians, let's check our work.

Characters: Harry, Ron, and Hermione in *Harry Potter and the Sorcerer's Stone.*

Desires: They want to prevent Lord Voldemort's return by finding and keeping the Sorcerer's Stone safe.

Conflict: Harry, Ron, and Hermione believe Professor Snape is working to steal the stone for Voldemort. They are faced with a wide variety of obstacles, including trying to find out what Snape is up to, how to get past what's protecting the stone, and, of course, the eternal challenge of how to avoid being caught by teachers and getting into trouble.

There you have it: our work checked out. Characters plus desires plus conflict does, in fact, equal story.

Unlike math, however, writing doesn't have an order of operations, so you can begin planning or plotting with whichever element makes the most sense to you.

There are many writers who say they begin with their characters because they are the heart of the story. Other writers say they know what's going to happen and then create characters to fit into the plot. And some writers say they begin somewhere in the middle—with the bare bones of a character and a vague idea of what's going to happen. In the end, no matter where these authors start, each of their stories will end up with characters, desires, and conflict.

So now the question is, where will you begin?

● EXPERIMENT WITH PLANNING OPTIONS

If you've ever written a story in school, your teacher most likely introduced you to (or, if we're being honest, required you to complete) a plot structure that looks like a roller coaster or a mountain or an upside-down check mark. Sound familiar? This traditional structure works well for many stories, but not for all of them. Similarly, there are plenty of writers who find the structure useful, and just as many who don't find it helpful at all.

Most novelists experiment with different approaches to planning and writing their stories until they find a method that's effective for them. To see what works for you, try one or all of the three fun and creative planning tools below. (The second option, which is marked with a *, is particularly well suited for plantsers and pantsers.)

Planning Igniter ❶
The Plot Roller Coaster

The *plot roller coaster*, also known as the plot mountain or Freytag's Pyramid, is a traditional plot structure that includes a setup, an inciting incident, some rising action, a climax, and a resolution. It has the shape of a roller coaster.

In addition to using a plot roller coaster to plan your story, you can also use it during the revision process to make sure you've covered each element.

Jump on and take a ride to learn more about each element of this method, using *Harry Potter and the Sorcerer's Stone* as an example.

>> The Setup (or Exposition)

The setup is a lot like the moment before you get on a roller coaster: you look around, see the landscape, and get a sense of the crazy ride you're about to go on.

In the setup of a story, we're introduced to the protagonist and the world in which they live. The setup typically takes the reader right up to the first moment of conflict, or the inciting incident.

In some books, the setup stretches across several pages, or even across a chapter, while in other stories, the setup is just a few sentences.

Here's the setup in *Harry Potter and the Sorcerer's Stone*: The first chapter introduces us to the protagonist, Harry, his aunt and uncle, and the "normal" world in which they live. The book begins, "Mr. and Mrs. Dursley, of number four, Privet Drive, were proud to say that they were perfectly normal, thank you very much. They were the last people you'd expect to be involved in anything strange or mysterious, because they just didn't hold with such nonsense."

>> The Inciting Incident

As the roller coaster launches forward, you know there's no getting off the ride. Your heart beats a little faster. Your palms begin to sweat. The adventure is just starting, and things are about to get wild.

Your protagonist has this same feeling when the inciting incident occurs. This moment of conflict launches them on their journey, and it makes the reader say, "Whoa, what's going to happen? I can't wait to read on!"

Here's the inciting incident in *Harry Potter and the Sorcerer's Stone*: After a series of escalating incidents where owls try to deliver Harry's acceptance letter to Hogwarts, Hagrid arrives in person, throwing us into the real story. "'Ah, go boil yer heads, both of yeh,' said Hagrid. 'Harry—yer a wizard.'"

▶▶ Rising Action

The ride up is filled with anticipation and suspense. Each passing second makes your stomach tighten and makes you grip on to the safety bar tighter (even though you're moving slowly). You know the big moment is just up ahead, and all you can think is: How big is the impending drop? What will it feel like to go down? Will the laws of physics save you or kill you?

The rising action in a story is made up of many events, all of them leading to the most exciting, or pivotal, part of your story: the climax.

Here's some of the rising action in *Harry Potter and the Sorcerer's Stone*: Harry Potter arrives at Hogwarts, a break-in at Gringotts Wizarding Bank is reported, and Harry sees Professor Snape in the Forbidden Forest with Professor Quirrell.

>> The Climax

You're only at the top of a roller coaster for a split second. There isn't enough time to take selfies with the incredible view behind you because in that quick moment, the only thing you can do is suck as much air into your lungs as you can. And then before you know it, you're shrieking on your way down.

The climax of a story is that highest peak, that moment of conflict the story has been climbing toward. The protagonist has faced many obstacles up to this point, but the climax is the biggest of all. This is the event the reader has been waiting for. It can be a big, loud event, like the final battle in a war, or it can be something smaller and quieter, like the arrival of a letter saying whether the protagonist has been accepted to the art school she's dying to attend.

Here's the climax in *Harry Potter and the Sorcerer's Stone*: ***SPOILER ALERT: If you haven't read the book yet, do NOT read the following paragraph.***

At last, Harry comes face-to-face with the

nemesis he's been chasing all book long, only to discover it isn't who he expected. He must overcome his enemy in order to secure the Sorcerer's Stone and prevent Lord Voldemort's return!

>> Falling Action

Without the crazy ride down, the highest point of a roller coaster wouldn't be nearly as exciting. The events that occur right after the climax make up the falling action and lead to the resolution.

Here's some of the falling action in *Harry Potter and the Sorcerer's Stone*: After the climax, Harry wakes up in the hospital wing in a panic, and neither he nor the reader is sure what happened. His conversation with Dumbledore acts as a bridge into the resolution of the story.

⨠⨠ The Resolution

Roller coasters don't come to a quick stop right after the big drop; instead, they coast for a bit, giving riders time to catch their breath and recover from the insanity they just endured.

The resolution of a story is the smooth ride to "The End"; it's when all of the loose ends are tied up.

Here's the resolution in *Harry Potter and the Sorcerer's Stone*: After Dumbledore explains what happened to Harry in the previous chapter, the main plot is resolved. Loose ends are then tied up at the end-of-year feast, and Harry's school year comes to an end.

Planning Igniter ❷
*What If?

What if modern-day scientists brought dinosaurs back and everything went wrong? That's the idea behind Michael Crichton's *Jurassic Park*.

What if everyone was born cursed and the color gray, but could be made beautiful by a select group of people? This is the idea behind Dhonielle Clayton's *The Belles*.

The simple question "What if?" is the starting point for every story. A story builds through a series of "what-ifs" because every story has to travel through many narrative forks in the road.

To get your story started—and to keep it moving forward if you're stuck later—use this exercise:

> ⏩ At the top of a clean piece of paper (or document, if you're typing), write "What If." Then let your imagination run wild and write down every "what-if" possibility you can think of. The wilder and crazier, the better.

Here are some "what-ifs" from author Neil Gaiman:

What if you woke up with wings? What if your sister turned into a mouse? What if you all found out that your teacher was planning to eat one of you at the end of term—but you didn't know who?

And here are a few creative ones written by NaNoWriMo Young Writers Program participants:

What if emotional scars showed on your skin?

What if a snowflake could capture all your memories?

What if private thoughts could be read by the public?

What if instead of money, you gave memories?

What if someone was living in that abandoned house?

If you already have your cast of characters figured out, try throwing them into your "what-ifs." For example, what if your protagonist snuck into the principal's office and got caught? What if your protagonist fell into a well and discovered a new world?

This isn't the time to adhere to logic, so kick out any Inner Editor who happens to be a stickler for the laws of reality. And don't worry if you write down a lot of what-if scenarios that you don't end up using in your story. Each "what-if" is a seed that contributes to your story (whether you use it or not), because the best way to get one great idea is to generate a lot of ideas.

Planning Igniter ❸
Your Story in Three Sentences

This planning technique is most effective when used to narrow down scenes or ideas you've already imagined into a simple structure. It's helpful to do the "What If?" activity before doing this one, so that you have a skein (that is, a loosely tangled ball of yarn) of plot possibilities.

To narrow your story to just the basics, take your ideas—all of the what-ifs—and sum them up in three simple sentences to plan your beginning, middle, and end. Here are two examples:

Cinderella

 Cinderella wants to go to the ball, but her stepmother won't let her.

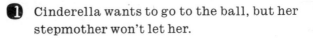 She goes anyway, meets the prince, and loses her shoe.

 The prince finds her and returns the shoe.

The Pied Piper

 A man lures rats away from the village.

 The village people don't pay him what they promised.

3 He steals the village's children.

Write the three sentences that summarize the action of your story on a sticky note and hang it above your desk to remind yourself of the structure of your story. You'll need to think about how to fill in the details from the first sentence to the second, and from the second to the third, but you've got the pillars of your story in place.

QUEST 4: BUILD YOUR STORY'S WORLD

Every story would be another story, and
unrecognizable as art, if it took up its
characters and plot and happened
somewhere else.... Fiction depends for its
life on place.   —Eudora Welty,
                    Pulitzer Prize–winning author

You Are Here

Setting is a character's gravity: it anchors them in
a specific time and place, allowing readers to see
the rickety bridge they're standing on, feel the
cold early-morning rain pelting their jackets, and
hear the fiery roar of a dragon flying overhead.

In some stories, the physical setting is just a
backdrop. It's the scenery around the characters

and the year (or time period) in which the story takes place. It keeps the characters from floating through the air, devoid of surroundings and context, but that's about it.

In other stories, the physical setting is as important as the characters themselves; in a way, the settings in these stories *are* characters. We get to know the land nearly as well as we know the characters plodding across it.

You don't need to decide what role the physical setting will play before you begin writing, but you should get to know the ins and outs of your characters' world before you transport readers there.

Take a look at this example and see if you can tell what's wrong with it:

> The sound of kids playing four square in her school's playground drifted into her bedroom, pulling her out of sleep. Skittle loved having her school so close to home— it was so close, in fact, that when her window was open, she could occasionally hear teachers sharing good gossip as they headed out for the night.
>
> As she was settling back into sleep, her

mom yelled, "Skittle, get your stuff and get in the car! We need to get you to school. Traffic is already bad, and you're already late!"

If the school is across the street from Skittle's house, why is her mom going to drive her there? Why does it matter if there's traffic? That doesn't make much sense. If you don't know your characters' world, your characters will have a hard time knowing which direction to go. And they might do silly things like drive across the street to school instead of walking.

To make your setting realistic, you should know where each character lives and where each building, park, school, and restaurant they go to is located. You should know whether the town, city, or planet has highways, dirt roads, or hoverboard lanes. You should know which flowers bloom in spring and what the air smells like in winter.

You might not include every detail in your story, but knowing your characters' world inside out and backward will help keep your characters grounded and your readers from feeling confused or lost.

Here's a great idea for visualizing your book's setting:

> For me, a book begins with a place. The feel
> of this place, its colors, its peculiar
> atmosphere—all of it has to be just right,
> especially early on in a new project.
> Whenever I start working on a new book, as I
> play around with the protagonist's voice and
> craft in the early chapters, I set up a
> dedicated image board. I then sift through
> hundreds of pictures on Pinterest, Flickr,
> Google, populating the board with images
> that make sense to the story I have been
> slowly building in my head.
>
> —Katya de Becerra,
> author of *What the Woods Keep*

DARE ⚡ MACHINE

World-Building: If you're creating an entirely new world or place in your story, there are a lot of things to take into consideration to make the setting feel as vivid and real as possible. Use these world-building questions to get started:

1 What is the population? (How many people—human or otherwise—live there?)

2 What is the power structure? (Who rules or is in charge?)

3 What is the climate? (Are there seasons? How does the climate affect inhabitants?)

4 What are the main geographic features? (Are there bodies of water, mountains, forests?)

5 How do inhabitants interact with the land? (Do they care for it? Destroy it? Use it for magic?)

6 What do characters eat? (And where does this food come from? How do characters access it?)

DARE ⚡ MACHINE

Zoom Out: Make a map of your story's setting. (Don't worry if drawing isn't one of your strengths—your map doesn't need to be a work of art, though it can be if that's your thing.) Give the town/city/planet a name. Label important places, like characters' homes, schools, buildings, and landmarks. Name streets, roads, physical features, and anything else that can be named. Be as detailed as possible.

Keep this map handy when you're writing (and update it as needed) so that you can refer to it as your characters move from place to place.

Zoom In: Choose four places from your map (for example, your protagonist's house, the river running through town, the diner across the street, and the protagonist's grandmother's house all the way across town). Describe each one in as much detail as possible, using all five senses (sight, sound, touch, taste, smell).

How's Your Mood?

A story's setting does more than paint a picture of the characters' surroundings—it also makes the reader *feel* something; it conveys a specific mood.

You feel the goose bumps rise along your arms as you see the protagonist making her way in the dark of night across the old cemetery, the very place where her best friend was murdered. You feel your heart rate slow and a sense of relief when she escapes the hands of a ghost who wants to steal her soul.

In movies, music helps set the mood for particular scenes, but in writing, it's often the setting that makes us feel particular emotions.

Take, for example, this passage from *A Wrinkle in Time*:

> It was a dark and stormy night.
> In her attic bedroom Margaret Murry, wrapped in an old patchwork quilt, sat on the foot of her bed and watched the trees tossing in the frenzied lashing of the wind. Behind the trees clouds scudded

frantically across the sky. Every few moments the moon ripped through them, creating wraithlike shadows that raced along the ground.

The house shook.

The author, Madeleine L'Engle, didn't just tell us that Margaret Murry was scared; instead, she showed us Margaret Murry wrapped in a quilt, in the attic, on a dark and stormy night. The words she chose to use to describe the setting make us feel like something ominous is about to happen. She also used a literary device called *personification*, which is giving human emotions or characteristics to something nonhuman ("clouds scudded frantically").

Imagine if the passage was written this way instead:

It was a bright and sunny fall day.

In her bedroom Margaret Murry, wrapped in a pink, fuzzy, cozy blanket, sat on the foot of her bed and watched the trees gently swaying back and forth in the crisp breeze. Behind the trees clouds

meandered across the sky. Every few
moments the sun poked through them,
creating shadows that skipped along the
ground.

The house hummed.

The mood in this passage isn't ominous anymore. Margaret Murry is in the same place—her
bedroom—but the time of day and description of
the weather change the feeling from scary to
carefree.

As you think about the setting(s) for your story,
consider the action (what's going to happen) in
each place and how you want your characters and
readers to feel.

DARE ⚡ MACHINE

Pulling a rabbit from a hat? Neat. But the trick you're about to do? Even cooler.

You are going to alter the mood of a particular setting by changing *just a few words*.

Start by writing a detailed description of a specific place in your story (for example, a classroom, a house, an alleyway, a swimming pool). Make the description convey an excited or happy mood. Think about how the place looks, smells, and sounds. Consider the time of day and the weather.

Now go back and replace the words that showed an excited or happy mood with words that convey a sad or depressed mood.

Finally, change the passage one last time to convey a scary mood.

Mirror, Mirror

Just as settings can create particular moods, they can also act as mirrors and reflect information about who characters are as people (or aliens or beasts or animals).

Let's take a quick look at Kelly's room to see what we can learn about her:

Kelly hadn't seen her bedroom floor in weeks. To get from her bed to her desk, she hopped down a path of old pizza boxes and books lined with hills of dirty (and probably clean) clothing. As she flipped through a pile of crumpled papers, she mumbled, "My homework must be in here somewhere."

We don't need to say "Kelly is a disorganized person," because her room *shows* us that she's a disorganized person.

DARE ⚡ MACHINE

What kind of person is your protagonist (for example, organized, scattered, creative, logical)? How about your antagonist?

Taking what you know about your protagonist, describe their bedroom in detail.

Now, taking what you know about your antagonist, describe their bedroom in detail.

WRITE!

You're ready. You're set. Now it's time to go forth and brave the page! To get started, you will make a progress tracker, kick your Inner Editor out of your life, and sign a contract pledging your commitment to writing your story your way. Then you'll make your way through your novel (or other writing project) using a week-by-week adventure map.

YOUR WRITING ADVENTURE BEGINS NOW

The time to tackle your big, audacious writing project is here! You might be heading into the wilds of your story with a detailed outline as your guide, or with only your burning desire to write lighting the path ahead. Either way, the only direction to go now is forward, transforming the blank page with your *who*, *what*, *where*, *how*, and *when*.

Part 3 is a week-by-week adventure map that will guide you through completing your novel, or any other creative writing project, in a month.* This map won't tell you what to write, but it will give you an ample supply of inspiration (including pep talks written by your favorite authors to begin each week), ideas for refueling when you're feeling stuck or exhausted, and tips for keeping your project on track.

We recommend reading each week's section

before you begin that week, so you know what you're heading into and how to prepare.

You'll find the following features for Weeks 1 through 4:

PACKING 🎁 LIST

(everything you'll need to stay warm, prepared, and inspired all week long)

TRAIL 💡 HEAD

(a place to learn additional craft techniques and find ideas for enriching your writing)

MOTIVATION ♻️ STATION

(an assortment of strategies to reinvigorate you should you fall into a metaphorical ditch along the way)

DARE ⚡ MACHINE

(a dare for each day of the week)

WRITER'S ☕ LAIR

(a quiet place to recalibrate and collect your thoughts)

---

* If your deadline is more or less than four weeks, you should adjust the amount of time you spend in each week of the adventure map. For example, if your deadline is seven days, go through each week in a little over a day; or if your deadline is two months, give yourself two weeks for each of the weeks in the map.

WEEK 0

⇨ PEP TALK ⇦
by Marissa Meyer

Dear Writer, you are facing a quest of mythic proportions. A daring adventure—rife with danger, yes, but also profound joy, the likes of which less daring individuals can never know. You, brave soul, are about to write a *novel*.

As you prepare to embark on this journey, you are probably facing a mix of emotions. You might feel elated at the prospect of filling blank pages with your words, and eager to start bringing your brilliant ideas to life. Or perhaps you're plagued with self-doubt. You might be worried that everything you write will be terrible and clichéd and boring. You might be afraid to fail.

This flurry of emotions is totally normal. And luckily, here in Week 0, you can use both the excitement and the uncertainty to set yourself up for a truly epic novel-writing month. Here are some things you can do to prepare for the task ahead:

Write down the things you already love about your story. Are you enamored with the unique fantasy setting? The devious villain? The star-crossed romance? What is it about *this* story that makes your fingers itch to get to the keyboard? Write it down now, so that if your motivation flags later, you'll have something to remind you about this loving feeling.

 Alternatively, if you're not yet sure *what* you're going to write about, no worries! Use this time to start a list of what you like in other novels—things like bank heists, bounty hunters, or creepy prophecies. Should you get stuck while writing, you can look at this list and remember, "Oh yeah, I like stories with buried treasure in them. Maybe there's a pirate map in this chapter!" And away you go.

 Brainstorm some challenges your protagonist could encounter. Don't be afraid to put your characters through tough times—that's where the suspense comes from! If it ever feels like your plot is dragging, you can pick a new obstacle to ramp up the tension.

 Create a story playlist. Even if you don't like to listen to music while you're writing, having a list of songs that put you in a creative mood can help spark new inspiration.

Visualize success. Close your eyes and picture yourself writing your novel. Not just writing, but having *fun*. Envision your fingers flying across the keyboard as ideas come pouring out of you. Then imagine how amazing you'll feel when you type those two glorious words: *The End*. Experience the sense of accomplishment, the pride, the knowledge that you did not give in to the doubts. You embraced the journey, you put words on paper, and *you*, amazing human being, wrote a *novel*.

Then open your eyes and know that in just a few short weeks, you will be experiencing that satisfaction for real.

Week 1 is approaching. Prepare to go forth and write!

· · · · · · · · · · · · · · · · ·

MARISSA MEYER is the #1 *New York Times* bestselling author of *Heartless* and the Lunar Chronicles. She lives in Tacoma, Washington, with her husband and twin daughters. She's a fan of most things geeky (*Sailor Moon*, *Firefly*, any occasion that requires a costume), and has been in love with fairy tales since she was a child. She may or may not be a cyborg.

The Eve of Your Adventure: Week 0

Before you head out on your journey, use Week 0 to finish gathering supplies, getting things in order, and reminding friends and family that you're going to be pretty busy for a while.

We know lots of people get pre-trip jitters (*What am I forgetting? What if I get lost? Remind me again why I'm doing this?*), so we've put together a handy checklist of everything you need to do to set yourself up for success before your imagination sets sail. If you haven't read Part 1 of the book yet, now would be a good time to go back and check it out, as it covers ways to set yourself up for success in great detail. And remember, success doesn't equal perfection. It means you've done what you set out to do.

(If you're raring to get started on your novel, the items on this list shouldn't take too long to complete; you can fly through them at your own pace and then leap into Week 1.)

1 If you haven't already:

> ✱ Activate your deadline.

> ✱ Set both your total word-count goal and your daily word-count goal. (There's a full explanation of how to do this in Part 1.)

2 Give your yet-to-be-written novel a title. (You can always change it later!)

3 Get crafty and make a progress tracker to chart your word count's upward movement. Marking how far you've come and the distance you have left to go will help keep you and your story on track. Plus, you'll get an awesome "I've got this!" rush every time you reach a milestone!

> ✱ What you'll need: poster board or a big sheet of paper, markers.

> ✱ Write your total word-count goal in a bright, bold color at the top of the page.

> ✱ Start with Milestone 10 and, working backward, list your milestones along with the word count you'll need to hit each one and the day you'll reach it.

> ✱ To calculate each milestone, divide your total word-count goal by 10. For example, if your goal is 5,000 words, you would need to write 500 words to reach your next milestone (5,000 words divided by 10 milestones).

✱ To determine how many days you'll need to write in order to reach each milestone, take the milestone and divide it by your daily word-count goal. For example, if you are writing for 30 days and your goal is 5,000 words, your daily word count would be 167 words (5,000 divided by 30). So the milestone is 500 words and your daily word count is 167; 500 divided by 167 is 2.99, but we'll round up and make it 3. It will take 3 days to reach each milestone. Here's what your progress tracker would look like:

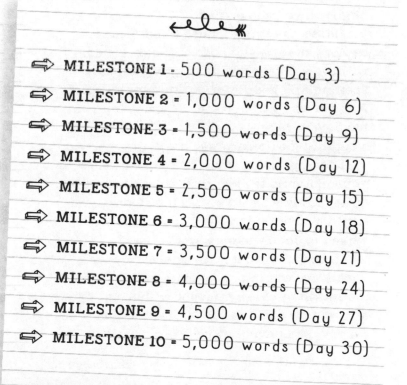

➡ **MILESTONE 1** = 500 words (Day 3)

➡ **MILESTONE 2** = 1,000 words (Day 6)

➡ **MILESTONE 3** = 1,500 words (Day 9)

➡ **MILESTONE 4** = 2,000 words (Day 12)

➡ **MILESTONE 5** = 2,500 words (Day 15)

➡ **MILESTONE 6** = 3,000 words (Day 18)

➡ **MILESTONE 7** = 3,500 words (Day 21)

➡ **MILESTONE 8** = 4,000 words (Day 24)

➡ **MILESTONE 9** = 4,500 words (Day 27)

➡ **MILESTONE 10** = 5,000 words (Day 30)

A Fond Farewell Party for Your Inner Editor

Dear Inner Editor,

You are cordially invited to a going-away party. For you. That's right, you're heading out. Shipping off. Where are you going? Anywhere that's far away from here. If I were you, I'd throw some suntan lotion in a bag and head to the beach. A little vacation might do you some good.

Here's the thing: I need to be free to explore, create, and soar through my draft without your incessant nagging about spelling and grammar buzzing in my ear. And I'm sorry if this sounds cruel, but I can't have your relentless need for perfection weighing me down while I'm writing.

I do appreciate your good intentions, and your meticulous attention to detail can be quite handy when it comes to revising and editing, so how about you come back home when I'm done with my story, okay?

In the meantime, let's celebrate your departure with your favorite meal: a mountain of cheesy nachos with a side of strawberry shortcake. (Okay, fine, that's *my* favorite meal, not yours.)

Bon voyage,
Me

If there's only one thing you do before you throw your first words down on the page, let it be this: Say farewell to your Inner Editor. Seriously.

DARE ⚡ MACHINE

Your Inner Editor's IQ might be off the charts, but it can't read minds, which means you'll need to be very clear and firm about your boundaries and need for space while you're working on your draft.

Follow these steps to get the message across to your Inner Editor loud and clear:

1 Close your eyes and picture your Inner Editor. What does it look like? Is your Inner Editor holding a dictionary or a ruler or something else to wave in your face when it's trying to get your attention? Have your Inner Editor say something to you ("Really, you're going to write a novel?"). What does its voice sound like?

2 Once you have a good mental image of your Inner Editor, grab a piece of paper and draw a picture of this nagging beast. Your drawing doesn't need to be a masterpiece; it just needs to capture the essence of your Inner Editor. (Your Inner Editor may try to scare you into thinking your picture isn't good enough, but guess what? It *is* good enough—now tell your Inner Editor to hush.)

Next, take the picture you drew of your Inner
Editor and throw a going-away party for it.
No, we're not talking about a big to-do with
lots of people and balloons and whatnot—this
party is just for you and your Inner Editor
and only needs to take a few minutes. Saying
farewell to your Inner Editor is a momentous
occasion, one that deserves to be celebrated
and honored. Grab your favorite drink or
snack, put on a celebratory (or ominous) tune,
take a deep breath, look your Inner Editor in
the eye, and tell it to hit the road.

4 When the moment is over, put your Inner
Editor somewhere out of sight, like in a
drawer you never use or in a shoebox in the
back of your closet. Don't get rid of it
completely, because as soon as you're
finished with your draft, you'll be happy to
welcome that little nitpicking voice home
again!

There's a well-known quote that begins, "You've
gotta dance like there's nobody watching. . . ."
With your Inner Editor away on vacation, your
imagination has permission to go wild and *write*
like there's nobody watching.

Daring Creator Contract

I, _____, hereby pledge my intent to brave the page and write a _____-word draft of a novel (or other writing project) in _____ days.

I understand that I am capable of heroic acts of creativity, and I agree to give myself enough time between now and my deadline to allow my innate gifts to come to the surface, untouched by self-doubt, self-criticism, and other acts of self-bullying.

During the month ahead, I will give myself permission to write my story the way I want it to be written. I believe my story matters, even if I decide not to share it with anyone. I will write with abandon and chuck any notion of perfectionism right out the window, where it will remain ignored until the editing process.

I acknowledge that upon successful completion of the stated writing objective, I am entitled to a period of gleeful celebration and revelry lasting days, if not weeks, afterward.

_____

YOUR SIGNATURE

_____

SIGNATURE OF TEACHER/PARENT/RELIABLE FRIEND

(Library Etiquette 101: Do not fill this out on the page if this is a library book! Instead, make a photocopy or type up your own contract at home.)

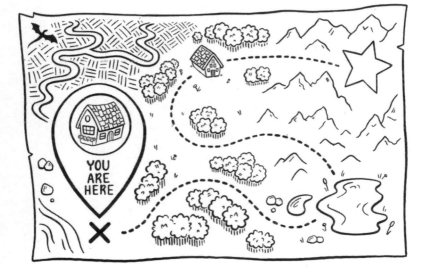

WEEK 1

⇨ PEP TALK ⇦
by Celia C. Pérez

When I was your age I thought my life, my home, and my neighborhood were beyond boring. And not only did my world seem as far from exciting as possible, but it looked *nothing* like the worlds I read about in books by my favorite authors. Beverly Cleary's Ramona Quimby never had to eat pig's feet in tomato sauce or translate English into Spanish for her parents. This was a big deal to me because it made me wonder if I could be a writer. What would I write about? Where did ideas come from? Was it okay to write about the things I saw in *my* world? What if my world just wasn't intriguing or mysterious or magical or cool enough to be worth writing about?

I want to let you in on a secret about writing. It took me a long time to discover this, and I wish someone had told me a little sooner. Are you ready? Okay, here it is: there is no prescription for finding ideas for stories or for being a writer. I know! Can you believe it? I always imagined there was something special writers did to be writers. Maybe they had magic pencils from a place only certain people had access to, like Diagon Alley! Maybe there was some kind of vitamin that filled them with ideas. Surely they lived in way cooler places than I did.

Once I figured out this wasn't the case, it was like I'd taken off a pair of sunglasses. When they were on, they shaded everything. But once they were off, I was able to see the full brightness of the world around me. Ideas came from experiences that I'd once thought were not good enough to write about, but also from objects and smells and feelings.

Stuck for ideas? Look up and look down. Look outside of your normal line of vision. What do you see? Do you notice things you didn't notice before? What kinds of stories are happening in the branches of the trees overhead? Who lives in the hollow in the old tree on your street? What is your librarian's secret identity? Anything around you—things, people, and places, even your day at school—can be the spark for an idea.

You have stories to tell that no one else can tell. It comes with being you and experiencing the world as only you can. Want to get started on your book? Start by taking off those sunglasses!

. . . .

CELIA C. PÉREZ is the author of *Strange Birds* and *The First Rule of Punk*, a 2018 Pura Belpré Author Honor Book, a 2018 Tomás Rivera Mexican American Children's Book Award Winner, and a 2018 *Boston Globe-Horn Book* Fiction and Poetry Honor Book. Originally from Miami, Florida, Celia lives in Chicago with her family, where, in addition to writing books about lovable weirdos and outsiders, she works as a librarian.

Where It All Begins
Week 1

Take one last look at that blank page in front of you.

What do you see? Nothing? A blank slate?

Perhaps. But what if all that *nothing* is actually *something*? What if your story is right there in front of you, but it's buried under a thick blanket of snow? Maybe it's shivering and cold and desperate for you to grab a shovel and dig it out. Or maybe your story isn't actually hiding in plain sight; maybe the blank page is actually a beacon, a bright light letting you know that your story is just ahead, waiting for you.

Whether you see the blank page as a warm invitation or a beast to battle, once you put your first words on it, it will transform into something new; it'll no longer be a blank page. And each new word you put down will be a step forward, a word closer to your goal, a word closer to "The End."

● WEEK 1

PACKING 🎁 LIST

* A novel-writing playlist with your favorite music to inspire and propel you forward (though writing in silence is okay, too!)

* A giant pile of super-healthy snacks like carrots and beets (we've also heard rumors that the occasional candy bar or gummy bear does wonders for one's creativity)

* A blank page (and a pen or a computer or whatever writing tools you plan to use)

* A comfy, private (if that's possible) place to write

TRAIL 💡 HEAD

··

Scary First Sentences and Why They Don't Really Matter (Yet)

Knock, knock.

Who's there?

Your story.

Your story who?

Your story who's ready to be written!

It's time to hurdle over that blank page and into your story—which, for some, isn't as easy as it sounds. We humans tend to be judgmental creatures, evaluating both what's in front of us and what's within us, which is why getting that first sentence of a story down can be challenging. We want to lead with something gripping and amazing and profound. We want those first marks on the page to be beautiful and perfect, like the opening sentences we collected from our favorite books in Part 1.

But guess what? Those first words don't really matter right now. There will be time later to go back and change them. There will be time later to make those first words everything you want them to be. Every one of our favorite novels started out as an imperfect and messy rough draft and went through multiple revisions to reach its perfect, polished state.

All that matters right now is getting started.

Sounds good, right? But even if you're not going for perfection, knowing *how*, exactly, to begin is a different story.

Here are a few ways to get your novel going.

>> The "There's No Turning Back" Moment

If you're looking for a surefire way to get things rolling, start with the very moment your protagonist's life changes forever (also known as the *inciting incident*). Beginning with the event that pushes your protagonist into action, and into their adventure or journey, is an example of starting *in medias res* (Latin for "in the middle of things"). Beginning smack in the middle of the action will hook your readers and pull them right into the story.

Take a look at the opening paragraph of *Where Things Come Back* by John Corey Whaley:

> I was seventeen years old when I saw my first dead body. It wasn't my cousin Oslo's. It was a woman who looked to have been around fifty or at least in her late forties. She didn't have any visible bullet holes or scratches, cuts, or bruises, so I assumed that she had just died of some disease or something; her body barely hidden by the thin white sheet as it awaited its placement in the lockers. The second dead body I ever saw *was* my cousin Oslo's. I

recognized his dirty brown shoes immediately as the woman wearing the bright white coat grasped the metallic handle and yanked hard to slide the body out from the silvery wall.

Whaley could have started the novel with lots of information about the protagonist and cousin Oslo, just to make sure we understood who the characters were, but that wouldn't have been nearly as intriguing as starting here, in the action, with two dead bodies. This opening leaves us with lots of questions (How did Oslo die? Were the protagonist and Oslo close? How will the protagonist react to the death of his cousin?), making it hard not to read on!

If you want to start with the inciting incident, something must happen to your protagonist that forces them to act. Your character could receive a mysterious letter, get into a fight, or forget to wear pants to school. Whatever it is that happens, your protagonist won't be able to go back to the way life was before. After the inciting incident, you can fill the reader in on all of the important details.

>> A Glimpse of the Setting or Environment

When the setting is so important to a story that it's almost like its own character (which is the case in many science fiction and fantasy novels), opening with a glimpse of the landscape can help pull readers into the story's world.

For example, J. R. R. Tolkien's *The Hobbit* begins:

> In a hole in the ground there lived a hobbit. Not a nasty, dirty, wet hole, filled with the ends of worms and an oozy smell, nor yet a dry, bare, sandy hole with nothing in it to sit down on or to eat: it was a hobbit-hole, and that means comfort.

Tolkien opens his book with a description of Bilbo Baggins's hobbit-hole. In just two sentences, we learn quite a bit about hobbits: they live in the ground, in holes; have furniture; and appreciate comfort. We also learn that we're heading into a world that's unlike our own—Tolkien's beginning pulls us right into a fantasy universe, in a fantasy story.

Using the setting or environment can be a fun and even powerful way to pull readers in. Beware, however, that if there's too much description right in the very beginning, you risk losing your readers' attention. If you're going to begin this way, try to fit the description into a few lines or a paragraph.

>> Hi, My Name Is . . .

Another way writers often start their stories is by having protagonists introduce themselves. Starting this way gives you a chance to share some important information about the character before jumping into the action.

Little Brother by Cory Doctorow begins:

> "I'm a senior at Cesar Chavez High in San Francisco's sunny Mission district, and that makes me one of the most surveilled people in the world. My name is Marcus Yallow, but back when this story starts, I was going by w1n5t0n. Pronounced 'Winston.'"

In this opening, Marcus is talking directly to us, the readers. He introduces himself not to tell us every detail of his life, but to bring us right to his story's starting place: when he "was going by w1n5t0n."

When you start with an introduction from the protagonist (or any character), be sure to reveal background information that will intrigue readers and is pertinent to your story's starting point.

>> Emergency Quick-Starters

If you've tried beginning with the inciting incident, the setting, and an introduction from your
protagonist, but the blank page still has a firm
hold on you, try starting your story with one of
these openers or prompts to loosen its grip.

Story Openers

* It was the worst day of [protagonist's] life. It
  all started when . . .

* Can you believe what happened to
  [protagonist]?

* This is the story of [protagonist].

* [Protagonist] was terrified of . . .

* [Protagonist] couldn't wait for . . .

* [Protagonist] swore it wasn't true.

* When [protagonist] woke up, everything
  looked different.

* Today is going to be a great day.

Prompts

* Start with a letter to the protagonist from the antagonist.

* Write the most absurd first line you can think of.

* Start with a joke.

* Begin with the protagonist stuck in an elevator.

* Begin with the protagonist stuck in an elevator with the antagonist.

* Begin with a fire. Or an earthquake. Or a loud explosion.

DIALOGUE

Dialogue is a conversation between two or
more characters.

You likely won't get very far into your story before
you realize your characters need to talk to each
other. (Your first line might even be one character
saying something to another.) When you add dialogue to your story, you (and your readers) hear
your characters' unique ways of speaking, which
gives you (and your readers) a better understanding of who they are as people and what their rela-
tionships are with each other.

Dialogue can also break up action or description passages, making your story easier to read—
and more interesting!

So this week, throw your characters into a
room (or an elevator, submarine, spaceship, or
whale's belly) and give them something to talk (or
yell or whisper) about!

Here are some tips for writing great dialogue.

Get to the Good Stuff and Move the Story Forward

When writing dialogue, it can be tempting to re-create real conversations—we want our characters to sound real, after all! But the things we tend to say in real life, like "Hi" and "Can't believe this weather," and also things like "um" and "uh" and "hmm," aren't all that interesting to read. For example, take a look at this dialogue:

"Hi," Dottie said.

"Hey," Jonah replied.

"I can't believe it's raining!" Dottie said.

"Right? I'm soaking wet," Jonah said.

Dottie looked around to make sure nobody was listening to them. Then, she leaned in close to Jonah and whispered, "Anyway, can you believe Mr. Typewriter got fired yesterday? I'm not supposed to know this, but I heard my mom on the phone last night, and she said that he stole money from the school!"

The first few lines might be realistic—it's polite to greet people when we see them, and it's hard not to talk about the rain when you forgot an umbrella—but they distract from the last thing Dottie says, which is what we *really* want to hear. Dottie's juicy news about Mr. Typewriter is significant and moves the story forward, which is what you want your dialogue to do.

Who's Talking to Whom?

When we talk to another person, we usually choose our words based on the situation and who we are speaking to. For instance, when talking to a teacher, you might ask, "Would it be okay for me to go into the hallway to do my work?" Whereas when you're talking to a friend, you might say, "Yo, I'm going to work out in the hallway. Holler if you need me."

When you're writing dialogue between characters, think about whom they're speaking to and which words they might choose for the situation.

He's Got Personality

You might not realize it, but the *way* you speak—
your tone of voice, word choice, and body language—
reveals a lot of information about who you are and
what you're feeling. Think about what your voice
sounds like and what your body looks like when
your teacher calls on you in class but you don't
know the answer to the question. Does your face
get red? Does your heart beat faster? Would you
mumble something like "Can you come back to
me?" or would you stand up, kick your chair, and
say, "I have no idea! And I didn't even raise my
hand!" Now think about how your response
reveals some of your personality traits. (For
example, the former reaction might show that
you're shy, and the latter might show that you're
prickly or hot-tempered.) When put in the same
situation, people with different personality traits
often react very differently.

When you're writing dialogue, use the way your
characters speak (their tone of voice, word choice,
and body language) to reveal and reinforce their
personality traits.

Take a look at the way Augustus speaks in this scene from John Green's *The Fault in Our Stars*. (A bit of context for this scene: The protagonist, Hazel, is in a support group for teens with cancer. Patrick is the leader of the group and the only adult in the room. Isaac has retinoblastoma, or eye cancer, and has just announced that he'll need to have surgery soon, after which he'll be blind. Augustus had "a little touch of osteosarcoma a year and a half ago," but claims to be in the support group at Isaac's request.)

> Neither Augustus Waters nor I spoke again until Patrick said, "Augustus, perhaps you'd like to share your fears with the group."
>
> "My fears?"
>
> "Yes."
>
> "I fear oblivion," he said without a moment's pause. "I fear it like the proverbial blind man who's afraid of the dark."
>
> "Too soon," Isaac said, cracking a smile.
>
> "Was that insensitive?" Augustus asked. "I can be pretty blind to other people's feelings."

Isaac was laughing, but Patrick raised a chastening finger and said, "Augustus, please. Let's return to you and your struggles. You said you fear oblivion?"

"I did," Augustus answered.

Patrick seemed lost. "Would, uh, would anyone like to speak to that?"

We learn quite a bit about Augustus by listening to what he says and the way he speaks. His quick responses show that he's confident, and his word choice tells us that he's intelligent, sarcastic, and unwilling or unable to talk about his feelings in that moment. Throughout the rest of the book, we hear Augustus use figurative language ("like the proverbial blind man who's afraid of the dark") and wordplay ("blind to other people's feelings"). His use of these devices is a part of his character and makes him unique.

Just like John Green did with Augustus, you can use your characters' word choice and styles of speaking to reveal information about what they're feeling in the moment and who they are as people.

Use this guide to figure out your characters' unique ways of speaking:

Word Choice: Are there any common phrases or words they use frequently? Do they use a lot of high-falutin (showy and pretentious) vocabulary words or crack a lot of jokes? Do they tend to speak in short sentences or longer ones?

Tone of Voice: Do they tend to speak clearly or mumble? What is their personality (serious, calm, enthusiastic, energetic, absentminded, easily discouraged, superficial, thoughtful, kind, etc.), and how does it affect the way they speak?

Social Interactions: Whom do your characters feel comfortable talking to? Whom do they open up to? Are there people your characters don't like speaking to, or people who make them nervous? What are their favorite topics to discuss? Are there people or topics they try to avoid at all costs?

Body Language: Do they tend to make particular facial expressions or gestures? Does their body language reflect how they're feeling and what they're thinking? Does their body language change when they're with certain people or talking about certain things?

Is *Said* Dead?

Dialogue tags are the words before, in the middle of, or after dialogue that let us know who's speaking. For example, in the sentence "'I love dialogue tags,' Margot said," "Margot said" is the dialogue tag.

While a seemingly simple concept, dialogue tags can cause quite a stir. Should you use *said* or should you find a more interesting word to let readers know who's speaking? Take a look at what Mrs. McDialogue thinks and see if you agree or disagree with her:

"Listen up!" Mrs. McDialogue said as she clapped her hands together three times. "I have some important news: the word *said* is dead. No need to sniffle; here's a list of three hundred words you can use instead," she said, hanging the poster in the front of the classroom.

You fidgeted in your chair. You looked around at the other students. Finally, you couldn't hold it in anymore and said, "But, Mrs. McDialogue, in all of the books I've read, the authors almost always use *said*."

Mrs. McDialogue pulled her faded red
handkerchief from her pocket and dabbed
her puffy nose. "I hardly think that's true.
Now get to work."

Classroom teachers want their students' writing to be descriptive and filled with a variety of interesting words, so they often encourage them to replace the dialogue tag *said* with words that are more colorful, more expressive. Understandable, right? Why say *said* when you can say *sneered* or *wheezed* or *blustered*?

Here's why: When you surround *what your characters are saying* with lots of extra words, it can be distracting and pull readers away from the heart of the dialogue. *Said* keeps it simple. *Said* lets the dialogue shine. So instead of telling readers that characters *growled* or *snarled*, use the action around their dialogue to show their emotions. For example:

Janelle crossed her arms and turned
away. "We're done here."
"You don't mean it," Roger said,
jumping to his feet.

In the first example, Janelle's actions (crossing her arms and turning away) replace the need for the dialogue tag *hissed* or *snarled*. And in the second example, Roger's reaction is implied in his words ("You don't mean it") and through his actions (jumping to his feet), so there's no reason to use the dialogue tag *whined* or *cried*.

If you're still unsure whether *said* is really dead, grab a few of your favorite books and check out their dialogue tags. Chances are, you'll see *said* is very much alive and well.

NOTE: It's fine to use interesting verbs as dialogue tags sparingly, and it's okay to use *asked* and *replied* every once in a while, too. If there were a dialogue tag food pyramid, it would look something like this:

BELLOWED

ASKED, REPLIED

SAID

MOTIVATION ♻ STATION

Help! I hate my idea!

You know the idea for your story? The one that seemed so brilliant in Week 0? At some point during Week 1, that scintillating idea might begin to lose its luster. It might even fade into a seemingly terrible and stupid idea that will never, ever work.

Unfortunately, self-doubt is one of the most dangerous roads to travel when you're writing a novel. If you continue down this road for too long, your writing—and your novel—will hit a wall and come to a complete halt.

Of course, starting over is an option. But if you allow yourself to start over now, there's a good chance you'll want to start over again tomorrow or in a week. And then guess what will happen? You'll keep doubting your ideas and starting over, and then a month will go by and you'll have a whole lot of beginnings but not one complete draft.

So if you find yourself questioning your idea, stop what you're doing, take a deep breath, and exhale slowly. Then try the following strategies:

Give yourself permission. Give yourself permission to doubt your ideas. All writers, at one time or another, have doubted their ideas, so why shouldn't you? Give yourself permission to write a "terrible" story (which is probably way better than you or your Inner Editor think it is). Give yourself permission to sit with the discomfort of doubting your ideas—a moment that often leads to a creative breakthrough—and then give yourself permission to get back to your writing. Look at this draft as a way to *practice* writing, rather than as a way to produce the perfect book. (And you never know, you may end up writing a great book in the process!)

Give your idea room to breathe. Instead of spending time trying to make your idea better, put it in a safe place, walk away, and spend an hour or even a day doing something else. Do the moonwalk. Meet up with a friend. Practice hanging a spoon on your nose. And then go back to that safe place, grab your idea, and start writing.

Give your idea some new flair. Sometimes all it takes to make an idea interesting again is a little spice, a little more flavor. Give your protagonist a new problem to tackle. Or introduce a new character who's full of self-doubt. Or move the story to a different location, like Mustafar or the Emerald City.

Here's a helpful tip from a fellow NaNoWriMo writer:

> If you start to hate your story idea, it probably has to do with an element of the story idea rather than the story idea itself. Maybe it has to do with one of your characters, or a particular occurrence that you had planned that isn't working out. Don't be afraid to stop and think it through!
> —Ailun, age 16

Help! My word count's going in the wrong direction!

There's one thing you absolutely cannot do if you want your word count to climb higher: remove words. Why? Because deleting words leads to *fewer words*.

What this means, of course, is that your novel will have words or sentences or characters or ideas you don't necessarily want or like. There's a chance that a few pages in, you'll realize your story should take place in New York City and not in Rome, Georgia, which would mean entire passages you've already written are *wrong*. Or you might find that your protagonist needs at least three siblings to make your story work, which means the entire section on being an only child is *wrong*.

This may seem like a major conundrum, but fear not, we have a win-win tactic for you: whenever you feel the desperate need to delete, *change the color of the text or highlight it instead.* Unhappy with a sentence? Make it blue! Description of a character off? Make it blue! Entire chapter that no longer works? Make it blue! Then, when you're done with your draft, you can revisit all of these blue (or whatever color you've chosen) words, sentences, and pages and delete or change them to your heart's content.

DARE ⚡ MACHINE

Monday: Pick a way to get started (in medias res, with the setting or environment, with an introduction from the protagonist, or using a story opener) and then . . . write!

Tuesday: Set a timer for 10 minutes and see how many words you can write in that amount of time.

Wednesday: Using dialogue, have one character lie to another to create tension.

Thursday: Write 150 words as quickly as you can. How long did it take? Next, write 300 words as quickly as you can. How long did it take?

Friday: Have a character break an object of great importance. Have a character break out in song in an unexpected place. Have a character break-dance. Have a character break down over something minor.

Saturday: Set a timer for 20 minutes and see how many words you can write in that amount of time.

Sunday: Make a list of everything that's in your protagonist's backpack or back pocket. Throw something unexpected in there. Then, using dialogue, have the protagonist explain the unexpected item to another character.

WRITER'S LAIR

....

Word Count Update

At the end of the week, check your word count to
see if you'll need to pick up speed in the next week
or if you'll have time to slow down and wander
through the wildflowers.

 What's your current word count?

 Are you on track? If you are behind or ahead,
recalculate your daily goal.

 Update your progress tracker.

Rearview Mirror

Take time to reflect on the week: What went well? What challenges did you face? Acknowledging the ups and downs of your writing life is an important part of the creative process.

Also, be sure to give yourself what you need to head into Week 2 with gusto and vigor. Do you need a rest? A run? An ice cream? Recharge so that you're ready to head into Week 2 at full steam!

WEEK 2

⇒ PEP TALK ⇐
by Jennifer Niven

Week 2 will be full of wonderful surprises, but chances are, it'll have some obstacles, too.

My mom (who was a writer as well) used to say that so much of writing is play, but sometimes we forget that because we get inside our heads and we get in our own way. We get frustrated and have trouble sticking with a story. We begin to doubt our ideas. If you experience any of these things this next week, remind yourself why you're writing this story to begin with. Ask yourself, "Why is this the story I chose to write out of all the other stories?" Try to get back to that initial feeling and inspiration you had. That's the thing that always helps me when I'm in the middle of a project and I start to doubt it. I remind myself why I'm writing it, why I wanted to write it in the first place, and then I also remind myself that this is a story I want to read and it's not going to be written unless I write it—then inevitably I get through the frustration and doubts and remember that *writing is play.*

Another challenge you might face this week is finding time to write—this is one of the biggest challenges a writer ever faces, because inevitably something or someone gets in the way of writing. Since you don't always have endless time to write, you have to carve time out where you can. My mom used to say to use the patchwork-quilt method of writing, which is something I've had to do many times. Here's how it works: you find time here, you find a little time there, you make time here, and then you gradually piece all of the bits together. It's not my preferred method of writing, but sometimes it's the only option.

Distractions tend to be more distracting once you're in a project—and there are so many ways to get distracted! Thankfully there are ways to keep motivated and to deal with those distractions, too. One of the things I do is wear my headphones to block everything out. If I'm really distracted and my mind is simply not cooperating, I put on music, and not just instrumental music or nature sounds, which is sometimes what I write to, but music with words. I find this loosens me up and gets me writing and I don't think about it as much; I don't overthink it and it helps me focus.

If an obstacle gets in your way this next week, just remember: writing is play.

....

JENNIFER NIVEN divides her time between Atlanta (where she was named one of *Jezebel*'s 50 Most Beautiful People) and Los Angeles (where her film *Velva Jean Learns to Drive* won an Emmy Award and she once played the part of Shania Twain in a music video). She has written nine books. When she isn't writing, Jennifer studies belly dancing, yoga, and electric guitar, and explores her inner bombshell. Find out more at JenniferNiven.com.

Welcome to Week 2

With a week behind you, your characters are starting to reveal their true selves and your story's plot is beginning to take shape. Writing for an entire week takes commitment, but writing for two entire weeks? That takes commitment *and* energy *and* passion.

Here's the honest truth: Week 2 will be *hard*. Your imagination will be tired and sore from flying through Week 1, and it will want a break. A long break. It will want to watch TV. And text with friends. And kayak down a river. And learn a new dance. And clean the bathroom. (Okay, it probably won't want to clean the bathroom.) It will want to do all the things that are not writing your story. Or your imagination might not want to do anything at all and will just flat-out refuse to come up with ideas.

But guess what? You're not going to let your imagination sing the Week 2 blues. Sure, this week may be challenging, but you're up for a challenge. You're committed and energetic and passionate. You can do this. *Your imagination can do this!*

As you push your story ahead this week, try to keep your protagonist from getting the thing they want most in the world too quickly.

You may know this already, but that protagonist of yours is eager and motivated, and if you're not careful, your character will sprint ahead to "The End" well before you've reached your word-count goal. To keep this from happening, you'll need to be a bit devious. A tad cunning. You may need to break some hearts or scream some nasty things. Week 2 isn't for the faint of heart, so don't be too nice to your characters.

This week, slow your protagonist down and stretch your story out by:

 Throwing lots of obstacles in your protagonist's way. As a writer, it's your job to stick it to your characters—to test them by putting them in all sorts of uncomfortable or dangerous situations. This will create conflict and build tension and suspense, which are the things that keep writers and readers interested and engaged (and squirming).

 Adding subplots. (You'll find more about subplots in this week's Trail Head.)

 Using description to pull readers into your characters' world.

● WEEK 2

PACKING 🎁 LIST

* An accountability partner or encouragement buddy whom you can call or text when you need a little pep, or some words of encouragement, or a good belly laugh.

* More super-healthy snacks, which some people call doughnuts and other people call cookies.

* A collection of postcards, old photographs, or travel magazines for inspiration.

TRAIL 💡 HEAD

· ·

Subplots

> *Subplots* are smaller story lines that are
> woven through and around the main
> events in a story. Sub means "underneath"
> (think of submarines), so subplots exist
> beneath the main plot, like a small story
> within a larger story.

One way to get started on creating subplots is
to zero in on those characters hanging around
your protagonist, like their friends and family
and teachers and therapists and ex–best friends
and mortal enemies. Even though these supporting characters aren't playing the lead role,
they should still be interesting and complex
and have their own voices and fears and desires.
By featuring your supporting characters in
subplots, you're developing those characters
further.

In *Harry Potter and the Sorcerer's Stone*, J. K.
Rowling uses subplots featuring Rubeus Hagrid,
the "Keeper of Keys and Grounds at Hogwarts," to

develop his character and push the main plot forward.

When he first vrooms into the story on his motorcycle, Hagrid sobs as he hands baby Harry to Dumbledore and Professor McGonagall. Despite his gruff, larger-than-life appearance, we learn that he's a sweet and loving giant (or technically half-giant, if you're a Harry Potter scholar) with good intentions. When he reappears in the story 10 years later, we learn that he's both loyal and not the best at keeping secrets, which are qualities that come in handy when Rowling needs a way to reveal information to Harry Potter and his friends—like when he accidentally tells Harry about Nicolas Flamel ("You forget that dog, an' you forget what it's guardin', that's between Professor Dumbledore an' Nicolas Flamel—").

To create a subplot for a supporting character, first decide what that supporting character wants most and then add conflict by dropping roadblocks in the way, just as you're doing in your main story line. (Make sure this new story line supports your story's main plot or one of the major themes; otherwise, it could be distracting or confusing!)

You can also use subplots to:

 Further develop the protagonist, settings, and themes.

 Show a different perspective.

 Change the mood or pace of a story.

Show, Not Tell (How Not to Be Captain Obvious)

Do you know people who deserve the name Captain Obvious? They're the ones who say, "Gee, the water in this hot tub sure is hot!" and "Wow, this zoo has a lot of animals!" They mean well, but everything a Captain Obvious tells us is self-evident and so . . . obvious!

Even if we don't view ourselves as a Captain Obvious in our everyday lives, as writers, it can be easy to morph into one without realizing it. We want to make sure our readers understand what's happening in our stories, so we think we need to tell them exactly what we want them to know: the water is hot; the protagonist is sad. But guess what? When we tell readers that a character is getting into a hot tub and the water is hot, or that a protagonist is sad because his girlfriend just broke up with him, we're stating the obvious!

So how can you make sure readers *see* and *feel* what's happening without explicitly *telling* them? You use description to create vivid images and scenes that *show* what's happening on the page.

A strong description is one that connects to your senses. When you *brush against the thorny bramble* and *wake in a fog of sweet gingerbread and cinnamon on Christmas*, you create a visceral connection with your readers, bringing them right into the story. In fact, there is even research that proves our brains react differently to words that are associated with smells (like *cinnamon* and *lavender*), textures (like *rough* and *bumpy*), and movements (like *kicked* and *sprinted*) than to nonsensory words.

Take a look at this passage from George Orwell's *1984*:

> Outside, even through the shut window-pane, the world looked cold. Down in the street little eddies of wind were whirling dust and torn paper into spirals, and though the sun was shining and the sky a harsh blue, there seemed to be no colour in anything, except the posters that were plastered everywhere.

Using sensory details, Orwell lets us *see* the weather. Instead of just saying "It was windy," he says, "little eddies of wind were whirling dust and torn paper into spirals."

But Orwell's intention isn't just to let us know the weather; it's also to create a feeling of unease. (Refer back to Part 2, page 75, for more about setting a mood.)

Here's another example:

> She looked completely different from everyone else. She was totally eccentric.

Can you get a clear picture of this eccentric character in your mind? What makes her different from everyone else? What does she look like? What's she doing? This passage tells us that the character is unconventional, but it's hard to feel connected to her because we can't picture her or the people around her.

Here's the *showing* version of that passage, from Jerry Spinelli's book *Stargirl*:

> And then I saw her. At lunch. She wore an off-white dress so long it covered her shoes. It had ruffles around the neck and cuffs and looked like it could have been her great-grandmother's wedding gown.

Her hair was the color of sand. It fell to her shoulders. Something was strapped across her back, but it wasn't a book bag. At first I thought it was a miniature guitar. I found out later it was a ukulele.

She did not carry a lunch tray. She did carry a large canvas bag with a life-size sunflower painted on it. The lunchroom was dead silent as she walked by. She stopped at an empty table, laid down her bag, slung the instrument strap over her chair, and sat down. She pulled a sandwich from the bag and started to eat.

Isn't it much easier to picture this character and her surroundings now? Spinelli used details to pull us into the lunchroom so that we could be there with the protagonist, watching Stargirl. He didn't tell us that Stargirl was eccentric, because he trusted us to figure that out on our own.

Description makes your writing more vivid, but this doesn't mean you should never use *telling* language. Telling works when you want to quickly explain something or summarize the weather, a setting, or an emotion in order to set the scene for more action or description. For example, in *Ready Player One*, author Ernest Cline first uses description to *show* us the narrator: "I was curled up in an old sleeping bag in the corner of the trailer's tiny laundry room, wedged into the gap between the wall and the dryer." And then he uses *telling* language to briefly explain why the narrator was in the laundry room: "I wasn't welcome in my aunt's room across the hall, which was fine by me." Had Cline shown us this information instead, we might have seen the narrator's aunt yelling at him to get out of her room, but that wouldn't have worked in this scene, and so simply telling us why he was in the laundry room works perfectly well here.

MOTIVATION ♻ STATION

Imagination Jump-Starters

When your imagination refuses to get out of bed, try jump-starting it with one or more of these activities:

 Doodle: grab a piece of paper and a pen and doodle for at least five minutes.

 Listen to music: turn the volume up high to get your imagination dancing.

 Try something new: eat a new food, try a new activity, listen to a new type of music, read a genre that's new to you. Find inspiration by getting out of your comfort zone.

 Build something: make something with LEGO or Popsicle sticks or paper clips or books or any other material you can find.

 Go outside and look around: observe the land, buildings, people.

>> Read a poem.

>> Write a poem.

>> Draw nine circles on a piece of paper and then make each circle into a different animal.

Deadly Distractions and How to Zap Them

Your mom has been screaming your name for 10 whole minutes? You haven't heard a thing because you've been floating through the rapids of your story. Your best friend sent 55 texts this morning? You wouldn't know because you've been deep in conversation with your characters. When words are flying from your fingertips, it's easy to block out the world around you.

Distractions, however, are always close by, lurking, waiting to pounce as soon as your fingers slow or your ideas stall or your characters stop talking back to you.

Distractions have a tendency to rise and attack like a zombie apocalypse during Week 2. To keep them from eating your brain, destroying your word count, and sucking the life from your story, you'll need to squash them as soon as they surface.

SOCIAL MEDIA (Facebook, Twitter, Instagram, Snapchat, Pinterest, and all other social platforms) and the Internet

This distraction looks like . . .

✳ Write a sentence or two of your story. Click over to YouTube for just a quick "peek." Watch a few videos for what you think is five minutes, except really 10 minutes have passed. Write a sentence. Read a blog post. Write a sentence. Post a selfie on Instagram. Write a sentence. Check to see how many "likes" you got on Instagram. With the entire World Wide Web just a click away, it can be tempting to sneak away for a quick bite of brain candy every few minutes, to see what's happening in the world and with your friends.

Ways to zap this distraction . . .

✳ Turn off your phone or put it in another room.

✳ Use an application or web browser extension to block social media or other distracting sites on your computer. There are a ton of options out there, with some allowing you to block sites by time of day or for a set chunk of time.

✳ Use a special text editing program on your computer that hides everything except your writing. To find one, search for "distraction-free text editors."

✱ Schedule time in your day for social media. Give yourself 30 minutes in the morning or evening to update your status, "like" photos, and post selfies.

✱ Use social media to help your writing. There are lots of great writing resources across various social media platforms, so if you find you can't keep away, use your social media time to get tips and ideas for your story. Here are some hashtags to explore: #WritingPrompt, #WriteTip, #WritingTip, and #NaNoWriMo. You can also use #WordCount to announce your word-count milestones and encourage other writers as they work to reach their goals.

YOUR INNER EDITOR

This distraction looks like . . .

✱ You're staring at your story, waiting for your
characters to do something, anything, when
all of a sudden you hear an ominous and
familiar voice whisper, "You know why your
characters are frozen on the page? Because
your story sucks. Might as well give up." But
wait! You sent your Inner Editor packing
before you started your story! How the heck did
it find its way back? Unfortunately, Inner
Editors are known to have an incredible sense
of direction, so every now and then yours might
pop in for a surprise visit.

Ways to zap this distraction . . .

✱ Turn off spell-check. It's okay for you to
misspell words in your first draft.

✱ If you're typing your story, try writing a few
pages in a notebook. Or if you're writing by
hand, try typing for a bit.

✱ Find an encouraging word or phrase and then
say it (repeatedly) to your Inner Editor. Here
are some ideas: "Writing is hard, and I can do
hard things." "It's fine for my first draft to be
bad; I can make it better later." "Inner Editor,
you have many wonderful strengths, but I'm
afraid writing a rough draft isn't one of them."

✱ If that doesn't work, be blunt. Tell your Inner
Editor to scram because this is your story and
you're going to write it your way.

✱ Sprint past your Inner Editor. Set a timer for
5–10 minutes and write as many words as you
can. Don't worry about spelling or
punctuation. Just. Write.

✱ Walk away. If telling your Inner Editor to
back off doesn't work, take a break from your
story. Scavenge for snacks. Surprise your
parents by cleaning your room. Play
tiddlywinks (or find out what tiddlywinks
are . . . and then include them in your story).

YOUR FAMILY AND FRIENDS

This distraction looks like . . .

✱ Your brother is desperate for you to play with
him. Your mom wants you to watch a movie
with her. Your best friend really needs to
FaceTime with you about her new crush.
Between your family and friends, it feels like
someone is trying to pull you away from your
writing every two minutes.

Ways to zap this distraction . . .

✱ Instead of leaving your story for your family
and friends, pull them into your story. You
can read one of your favorite passages aloud,
tell them about what your characters are up
to, or talk through some of your writing
challenges. You might not be adding to your
word count, but talking about your story with
another person can be a huge help with
generating new ideas and working through
issues.

✱ Use your calendar to schedule time for writing
and time for family and friends. Share your
schedule with the important people in your life
so they know when you're free to hang and
when they should leave you alone with your
writing.

Organize a writing party. This is a great way to spend time with the people you care about while simultaneously boosting your word count. Invite people to your house and ask them to bring their favorite writing snacks, or plan a meet-up at your local library or coffee shop.

Help! My word-count goal is way too high and I'll never be able to reach it!

Have you ever heard the saying "your eyes are bigger than your stomach"? Sometimes we go after big goals because they seem achievable in the moment, only to realize we bit off more than we could chew—like how eating an entire cake might sound like a great idea at first, but two slices in, your body may tell you otherwise.

This phenomenon happens with word-count goals, too. Maybe setting a super-high goal made sense in the moment—because writing is fun, and you have lots of free time, and your friend chose a high goal so you figured you should, too! But now, in Week 2, you've come to realize that you don't have *quite* as much time as you thought you would, and who really cares what your friends' goals are? If your once-tantalizing word-count goal is now making your stomach hurt, fear not: you can take a smaller portion. Lowering your word-count goal is absolutely okay—what's not okay is giving up!

Moral of the story: If you need to lower your word-count goal to make it more manageable, go for it. But whatever you do—keep writing!

DARE ⚡ MACHINE

Monday: Go on a subplot search by looking for them in TV shows and books. Keep a record of your favorites.

Tuesday: Create a subplot to reveal information about your protagonist by having them help a supporting character in some way.

Wednesday: Create a subplot by having a character who had moved away return unexpectedly.

Thursday: Find a postcard, an old photograph, or a photo from a magazine that shows a particular place or landscape. Set a timer for 10 minutes and then describe what you see in the image in as many words as possible.

Friday: Enter a character in an eating contest. Describe the scene using all five senses.

Saturday: Make a list of smells that trigger your memories or emotions. Think about smells associated with holidays, a family member (like the shampoo your dad uses or your mom's perfume), or activities (like a campfire or woodshop). Next, make a list of scents that elicit strong memories from your protagonist's past. Begin a scene with one of the scents and describe your protagonist's reaction.

Sunday: Give one of your characters an imaginary social media account (for example, Facebook, Twitter, Pinterest, Instagram, etc.). What do they post? Who sees their posts? Have this character look at a different character's social media page or feed—what do they see?

WRITER'S ☕ LAIR

....

Word Count Update

At the end of Week 2, check your word count to see if you'll need to pick up speed in the next week or if you'll have time to relax and maybe even see that new movie with your friend.

    � **✳** What's your current word count?

    ✳ Are you on track? If you are behind or ahead, recalculate your daily goal.

    ✳ Update your progress tracker.

Rearview Mirror

Take time to look back on the week: How was your energy level? What made you really excited? What brought you down? Remember that acknowledging the ups and downs of your writing life is an important part of the creative process.

Before you head into Week 3, do three kind things for yourself: stretch your fingers, have a private dance party to get the blood moving through your body, eat a super-healthy meal to give your body extra fuel for the upcoming week, or do something else that will make you happy. Writing is intense; a little self-care will go a long way.

WEEK 3

⇒ PEP TALK ⇐
by John Green

Way down deep in the dark archives of my hard drive, I have a folder called Follies, which contains an impressive collection of abandoned stories: there's the zombie apocalypse novel about corn genetics, the sequel, the one about the Kuwaiti American bowling prodigy, the desert island novel, and many more. These stories have only one thing in common: they're all about 25,000 words.

Why do I quit halfway in? I get tired. It's not fun anymore. The story kind of sucks, and it's hard to sit down every day and spend several hours eating from a giant bowl of suck. And most of all, like the kid who spends hours preparing plastic armies for war, I enjoy setting things up more than I enjoy the battle itself. To finish something is to be disappointed. By definition, abandoned novels are more promising than completed ones.

You have likely reached the moment in this

insane endeavor when you need a rock-solid answer to the question of why, precisely, you are trying to write a novel in a month. You have likely realized that your novel is not very good, at least not yet, and that finishing it will be a hell of a lot less fun than starting it was.

So quit. Quit now, or if you're among the many of us who've already quit, stay quit. Look, we are all going to die. The whole species will cease to exist at some point, and there will be no one left to remember that any of us ever did anything: our creations, all of them, will crumble, and the entire experiment of human consciousness will be filed away, unread, in the Follies folder of the great interstellar hard drive. So why write another word?

Sorry. I reached the halfway point of this pep talk and tumbled, as one does, into inconsolable despair.

Here's my answer to the very real existential crisis that grips me midway through everything I've ever tried to do: I think stories help us fight the nihilistic urges that constantly threaten to consume us.

At this point, you've probably realized that it's nearly impossible to write a good book in a month. I've been at this a while and have yet to write a book in less than three years. All of us harbor secret hopes that a magnificent novel will tumble out of the sky and appear on our screens, but almost universally, writing is hard, slow, and totally unglamorous. So why finish what you've started? Because in two weeks, when you are done, you will be grateful for the experience. Also, you will have learned a lot about writing and humanness and the inestimable value of tilting at windmills.

Something else about my Follies folder: it contains the final drafts of my novels *Looking for Alaska*, *An Abundance of Katherines*, and *Paper Towns*. They are follies, too—finished ones. Whether you're reading or writing, there is nothing magical about how you get from the middle of a book to the end of one. As Robert Frost put it, "The only way out is through."

So here's the pep part of my pep talk: go spit in the face of our inevitable obsolescence and finish your novel.

JOHN GREEN is the award-winning, #1 bestselling author of *Looking for Alaska*; *An Abundance of Katherines*; *Paper Towns*; *Will Grayson, Will Grayson* (with David Levithan); *The Fault in Our Stars*; and *Turtles All the Way Down*. His many accolades include the Printz Medal, a Printz Honor, and the Edgar Award. John has twice been a finalist for the *LA Times* Book Prize and was selected by *TIME* magazine as one of the 100 Most Influential People in the World. With his brother, Hank, John is one half of the Vlogbrothers and co-created the online educational series CrashCourse. You can join the millions who follow him on Twitter @johngreen and Instagram @johngreenwritesbooks or visit him online at johngreenbooks.com. John lives with his family in Indianapolis, Indiana.

You've Arrived at Week 3

You've made it through two wild weeks of writing. Know what that means? You've made it to the half-way point! (*gives high five*) Sure, there's still a good amount of distance between you and "The End," but if you can write for two weeks, you can definitely write for another two. Pat yourself on the back and then slide on into the second half of your writing adventure.

During Week 3, you'll want to:

✱ Push your protagonist to your story's peak, the climax (so raise the stakes with obstacles—even punish your protagonist).

✱ Begin to tie up loose ends and subplots.

At this point in your journey, if you're halfway or a little over halfway through your story, you're right on track.

If you're nowhere near the middle, don't worry, you still have time. Here's what we recommend you do:

1 If you have an outline or story map, take a look at it and see which scenes or events you can skip or shorten to get your protagonist closer to the climax. You can flesh them out when you revise.

2 If you don't have an outline or story map, making a quick one now will help you see what your protagonist needs to do in the next two weeks.

● WEEK 3
PACKING 🎁 LIST

✳ Writer's Block Spray, SPF 100

✳ A mantra or saying to help you power through the middle (for example, "I've made it this far, and I know I can make it to the end!" or "I'm not going to give up, because my characters deserve an ending!")

✳ Mud boots to help you slosh through the middle of your story

TRAIL 💡 HEAD

···

Sudden Twists and Unexpected Turns

You know when you're reading a book and the plot seems to be heading in one direction but then all of a sudden—bam!—something changes or is revealed and the entire story completely shifts and you're left wondering how you didn't see it coming? Those unexpected turns in a story are called *plot twists*. Finding out Darth Vader is Luke's father in *Star Wars: Episode V*? That was a shock when the movie first came out! We won't give any more spoilers, but here are a few examples of books with big surprises: *We Were Liars* by E. Lockhart; *Everything, Everything* by Nicola Yoon; and *Looking for Alaska* by John Green.

A plot twist is a great tool to use when you want to add tension or an element of surprise to your story. You can also throw one into your writing if you're stuck or feeling like your story is becoming a bit dull or predictable.

Here are several types of plot twists you can test out:

Untrustworthy or Unreliable Narrator Someone is telling the story, and up until now, we haven't had a reason to doubt this character. But in a sudden reveal, we learn something that makes us question everything this character has told us thus far.

For example, let's say we believe your protagonist when she says she remembers the morning of her fourth birthday, the day her mother gave her up for adoption, which is why she lives with Nina, the woman who took her in (and who desperately wants the protagonist to call her Mom), and why, 10 years later, she's on a quest to find and reconnect with her biological mom. But then, in a sudden reveal, we learn that your protagonist suffers from delusional disorder, a mental illness that makes it hard for her to tell what's real and what's imagined. We also learn that Nina is in fact her biological mother and that she was never given up for adoption. All of these things make the protagonist unreliable. (*Unreliable* doesn't necessarily mean *bad*; it just means that the character's story is questionable.)

Unexpected Death or Missing Person In an unexpected turn of events, an important character dies or vanishes, shocking your readers and pushing your story in an entirely different direction.

For example, perhaps your protagonist and his brother are in a band together. We've gotten to know both these characters well, and we're excited to see what kind of mischief they'll get into on their big world tour. But then, the night before their flight to Paris, the brother disappears. All of a sudden, this is no longer a story about two brothers traveling with their band.

(Word of advice: While it would be unexpected, don't kill off your protagonist, as your readers are attached and invested in this character.)

Discovery or Recognition Shocking both readers and the protagonist, a character's true identity is revealed.

Maybe everyone is on edge because there's a killer roaming the streets of your protagonist's town. Your protagonist, her mom, and her mom's boyfriend have taken every precaution to protect themselves and their home. So the moment your protagonist realizes her mom is the killer? Mind-blowing.

(In order for a plot twist to really work, there should be subtle evidence sprinkled throughout your story, but nothing too obvious. You don't want your readers to see the twist coming. For example, if we see the mom cleaning blood off her shirt and then hear her talking about how she can't control her impulses, we're not going to be that surprised to learn she's the killer!)

A twist can also lead to a protagonist learning the truth about their own identity. Perhaps your protagonist is going after the title "World's Youngest Person to Swim the English Channel," and so far she's not only trained tirelessly along-side Daniel Lee, the first teenager to swim the channel, but has also overcome her fear of sharks through intense hypnosis. A week before her big swim, she discovers a photograph revealing that she's actually part mermaid.

Plot twists can be a fun way to shake things up—both for your readers and for you as a writer!

A Well-Balanced Story: Action, Description, and Dialogue

If we ate chocolate for every meal, we might be psyched at first—chocolate cereal, chocolate sandwiches, chocolate noodles!—but, alas, eventually we wouldn't feel very well. We also wouldn't feel very well if we only ate apples, even though they're considered a healthy food. In order for our bodies to feel great, we need to eat balanced meals with a variety of foods.

Novels are similar—they, too, benefit from balance and variety. A book that's all action would be difficult to keep up with. And a book that's entirely made up of description would be hard, and probably boring, to read. In order for a book to be balanced, it needs a combination of action (or movement), description, and dialogue. Interspersed, these three elements keep readers engaged and stories moving forward.

Take a look at this short example from Philip Pullman's *The Golden Compass*:

Lyra reached the dais and looked back at the open kitchen door, and, seeing no one, stepped up beside the high table. The places here were laid with gold, not silver, and the fourteen seats were not oak benches but mahogany chairs with velvet cushions.

Lyra stopped beside the Master's chair and flicked the biggest glass gently with a fingernail. The sound rang clearly through the hall.

"You're not taking this seriously," whispered her dæmon. "Behave yourself."

Her dæmon's name was Pantalaimon, and he was currently in the form of a moth, a dark brown one so as not to show up in the darkness of the hall.

Pullman uses a combination of action, dialogue, and description to pull us into the story, keep us engaged, and move the plot forward.

The action in the scene shows us what's happening: we see the protagonist, Lyra, sneaking into the dining room and flicking the glass with her fingernail. From Lyra's actions, we know she's doing something she's not supposed to be doing, and we're scared she's going to get caught. This conflict creates tension and pushes the story ahead.

Through description, we're able to see the fancy gold silverware on the table and the mahogany chairs with velvet cushions. We're also able to see that Pantalaimon is a dark brown moth.

The dialogue, which is sandwiched between the action and description, provides a nice pause, making the scene easier to read. It also gives us insight into both Lyra's and Pantalaimon's characters: Lyra is mischievous, and Pantalaimon is more serious and cautious.

As you're writing this week, try to include action, description, and dialogue in your story. You don't need to have all three elements on every page, but if you find yourself with long sections of description, or an entire chapter that's only action, or lines upon lines of dialogue, switch to one of the other elements.

MOTIVATION ♻ STATION

Writer's Block

Your story is in front of you, you're ready to write, but your mind is blank. You call out to your imagination, "Help! I need you!" but there's no response. You stare. And stare. And stare. But no matter how hard you try, you can't seem to get a single word down. You try going for a walk. You try talking to a friend. You try screaming into a pillow. But still the words won't come.

If this scenario sounds familiar, you, dear writer, have a case of writer's block.

The good news is that this diagnosis isn't fatal. Your story will survive! Just take one or more of these over-the-counter remedies to get your ideas flowing again:

Grab your writer's block and give it a great, big hug. Don't try to fight or hide it, because that will make it worse; instead, accept that you're stuck. And then acknowledge that all writers (including the most famous ones) face this challenge.

Next, tell yourself that there's a way to unclog your ideas. You might not have found it yet, but it's out there. Learning to honor and accept these creative impediments will help you see them for what they are: a part of the beautiful and sometimes angst-ridden creative process.

Write through your block. Write nonsense. Write what you had for breakfast. Write about how you hate not knowing what to write. Your words might not make sense. They might not relate to your story. They might feel like a waste of time. But eventually, the very act of writing will shake your imagination out of its deep slumber and you'll find that you've landed back in your story.

Talk it out with another person. Call a friend or corner a family member and tell them you can't think of what to write next. Give them a rundown of your plot or a brief summary of the last scene. Talking about your story with another person can help generate new ideas and enthusiasm.

Talk it out with your Inner Therapist. That's right—next to your Inner Editor's office is your Inner Therapist, a licensed practitioner who loves to listen and help solve complex problems. Here's how it works: you ask questions, and then write down your Inner Therapist's responses. Take a look at this example:

ME: Why can't I think of what to write next?

INNER THERAPIST: That's a great question. I wonder if you could try to answer it yourself. Why might you be having a hard time thinking of what to write next?

ME: Let's see. My protagonist is stuck in jail, so there's not a lot she can do. I feel like I backed my story into a wall. Or into a cell. Now nothing can happen.

INNER THERAPIST: Interesting dilemma! I wonder why nothing can happen in jail. What does she think of the food? Do prisoners ever get food poisoning? Is your protagonist going to try to escape? Or does she meet any other prisoners? What if there's a prisoner who looks just like her? Or like her mom? Or grandmother?

ME: Those are good questions. I like the idea of her seeing someone who looks like her. Thanks!

Meet with your mentor. Remember that mentor of yours, the one who's available 24-7 and totally free of cost? That's right—we're talking about your favorite book. Take some time to flip through it. Reread your favorite parts, or read a random page or two. How does the author push the story forward? What are the subplots in the book? Are there any plot twists? Remember, you should never copy another person's work, but you can definitely take ideas and make them your own. For example, let's say the protagonist in your favorite book loves to spy on strangers; you could then have your protagonist spy on a friend or family member. Or let's say there's a chapter in your favorite book that's told entirely in verse (poetry); you could try writing a chapter of your story in verse.

DARE ⚡ MACHINE

Monday: Enter into a Word War with a friend or against yourself. Directions: set a timer for 15 minutes and see how many words you can write. Who wrote more, you or your friend? If you're going against yourself, set a timer for another 15 minutes and see if you can beat your last word count.

Tuesday: Add a twist to your story by destroying an important building or landmark (using fire, a natural disaster, dinosaurs, a science experiment gone wrong, or something else entirely) in the place where your protagonist lives.

Wednesday: One of your characters flees or runs away. Why did they leave? Where do they go? What do they discover?

Thursday: Have one character write a letter to another character. Have a character receive a letter.

Friday: Add a cat to your next scene. Set a timer for 10–20 minutes and write as many words about that cat as you can.

Saturday: Give a character a phobia (an extreme fear of something). Here are a few phobias to consider: fear of spiders (arachnophobia), fear of crowded spaces (agoraphobia), fear of heights (acrophobia). How does the character handle their phobia?

Sunday: Add a twist to your story by revealing that a character is unreliable. Was everything the character told us a lie? How does this affect the protagonist?

WRITER'S ☕ LAIR

Word Count Update

Check your word count. Are you where you should be? Are you ahead of the game? Taking a moment to recalibrate will help keep you on track.

 What's your current word count?

 If you are behind or ahead, recalculate your daily goal.

 Update your progress tracker.

Rearview Mirror

Look through your work and find a passage or paragraph that you love (but no editing as you're looking!). What's working well in your story? What's not working so well?

Before you climb into Week 4, take a quick break—maybe soak your feet (and fingers) in a nice, hot bath; cook a meal with a friend; explore nature; decorate your room; or do something else that brings you joy.

WEEK 4

⇒ PEP TALK ⇐
by Danielle Paige

By Week 4, you know your world, and your characters are "talking to you." You've been meeting your daily word count. You've done all the heavy lifting. All that's left is getting to "The End" or "Happily Ever After" or "Not So Happily Ever After." So why is it so hard to get to that last page?

If you're an outliner like me, you've known the end of your story before you put pen to paper or fingers to keyboard. But somehow this week you find yourself staring at the blank page or blinking cursor.

First up, know that you are not alone. The slow-down before the finish line is something that lots of writers experience, from bestselling authors to first-time novelists.

When I was finishing the first draft of *Stealing Snow*, I found myself stuck. I knew exactly what I wanted to happen, but for some reason I kept re-writing the same three chapters wherein my Snow

Queen is betrayed by someone she loves and there are deadly and icy consequences. Finally, I called one of my dearest writer friends, Kami Garcia, and I talked it out. And in the process, I realized that my problem wasn't that Snow kills someone; it was *whom* she was supposed to kill that was holding me up. The betrayal was not big enough for her fatal action. I adjusted the plot and rewrote the chapters in a single night. And ultimately, Snow killed a more worthy adversary.

The reason I stalled is because something was in my way: my own plot. Once I removed that obstacle, I could get back on track and cross the finish line.

So how do you figure out what your own personal roadblock is?

Start by rereading the manuscript to pinpoint what your characters' motivations are. Ask yourself if there's another version of the ending that you want to try. If you can't figure it out on your own, ask a friend.

But what if the problem isn't on the page? What if it's in your head? Writing, for all the joy it brings, can be a little bit scary. Sometimes when you get close to the end, you start to think about what comes next. What will other people think when they read it? Will I ever get an agent? Will I ever get published? Sometimes the hardest thing to do in the last pages is to stay present in those pages.

So let yourself off the hook. No one's first draft (not even Neil Gaiman's) comes out perfectly; that's what revision is for. But first you need to finish it, so there is something to revise. The finish line is really another starting line.

....

DANIELLE PAIGE is a graduate of Columbia University and the author of the *New York Times* bestselling Dorothy Must Die series. Before turning to young adult literature, she worked in the television industry, where she received a Writers Guild of America Award and was nominated for several Daytime Emmys. She currently lives in New York City.

Enter the Great Fortress of Week 4

It was the best of weeks. It was the worst of weeks.

Week 4 is all about extremes: extreme stress, extreme work, extreme motivation, extreme exhaustion, extreme exhilaration. It's the hardest and easiest week of all.

You can finally see "The End" glistening up ahead, waiting for you to grab it. You can imagine holding it over your head and parading through the streets, screaming, "I wrote a novel! An entire novel!" When the wind blows in the right direction, you can smell hints of the sweet aroma of typing that last word. But even though you're *so* close, you still have words to write and loose ends to tie up before you reach your goal.

During Week 4, the power of your deadline will really come in handy. If your word count is lagging and you've had a hard time finding the motivation to write, summon your deadline to remind you that time is running out. Once you hear its mighty voice, you'll start cranking out the words. Or if your characters have been slowly plodding along and aren't anywhere near resolving their conflicts, harness your deadline to help get them moving.

Getting started on a novel (or other writing project) is hard. But finishing it is even harder. It's also the most important thing you can do as a writer—finish your projects.

Your goals during Week 4 are to:

>> Write your story's resolution (ending).

>> Reach your final word-count goal!

⊕ WEEK 4

PACKING LIST

✳ String to tie up those final loose ends

✳ A recording of Queen's "We Are the Champions," or a different song to push you to the end

✳ Your party shoes, for doing your victory dance

TRAIL 💡 HEAD

··

Writing Your Story's Ending

Beginnings are first impressions, and endings are what we remember.

Books we love have happy endings, devastating endings, and totally shocking endings. Books we love leave us feeling satisfied in some way; they give us a sense of closure by resolving the major conflicts. Books we're meh about? They often have endings that leave us saying "Really? That's it?" or "Wait, we never found out what happened!"

This might sound like a lot of pressure, but here's some good news about your ending: it doesn't have to be great or perfect or satisfying right now. (Yes, we've said this before, and we'll continue reminding you, because perfection can be enticing—another thing we've said before!) You can fix it up and make it all of those things during the revision process. In fact, Ernest Hemingway rewrote the ending to his famous novel *A Farewell to Arms* dozens of times. Right now, all that matters is pushing yourself and your characters to a final destination.

What might that final spot look like? Here are a few ideas:

All Resolved: Wrap up all the major conflicts and subplots with a nice, glittery bow (or some twine or floss or whatever string you have handy).

Plot Twist: End with a big, sudden twist. Have a character turn out to be someone (or something) else entirely. Or have the protagonist realize or reveal that their world—or their understanding of their world—isn't quite aligned with reality.

Happily Ever After: You can write a fairy-tale "Happily Ever After" ending, or you can simply end on a happy, positive note that leaves readers saying "Aww." (Just be sure to resolve the major conflicts and deal with loose ends!)

Back to the Beginning: End by putting your protagonist right back where they started. If your story opens with your protagonist blowing giant bubbles off the roof of their house, end with your protagonist popping one of those bubbles (oh, the symbolism!).

However you choose to end your story, make sure to:

    ✱ Resolve major conflicts.

    ✱ Tie up important subplots.

    ✱ Show how your protagonist has grown.

MOTIVATION ♺ STATION

··

There's no way I'm going to reach my word-count goal by the end of the week! Should I quit now?

No! Sure, it would be nice for you to reach your goal, but your goal isn't really why you're here. You're here because you have a story to tell, and that story needs an ending. Quitting now would be like baking a cake but forgetting to put the icing on. Or training for a marathon and then oversleeping on the big day. Or rescuing a drowning person only to desert them in a rowboat in the middle of the ocean.

Save that person in the rowboat by writing the ending! Don't give up on your story. And don't freak out if you don't reach your word-count goal. This is only practice for your next draft, after all.

Here are some wise words from NaNoWriMo participants who didn't meet their goals:

I have participated in NaNoWriMo for two years. The first year, I reached my goal, and the second year, I didn't. Even though I didn't reach my goal, I still had a blast writing my novel! I remember one weekend, I stayed up all night writing, because I had so many ideas flowing and I just had to get them down!

—Cassie, age 16

I took my love of writing a step further and pushed the limits; it was wonderful. I may not have reached my goal, but it's a work in progress: I'll get there eventually. It could take years, but I'll take my writing passion and make it into a writing talent, and you should do that, too.

—Alice, age 10

I *started* a story, and it was my own. I felt successful. I felt like I had done something instead of nothing. And it was *fun* to write, even if I didn't reach my goal.

—Bianca, age 14

I'll definitely hit my word-count goal, but there's no way I'll be able to finish my story by the end of the week!

It's fantastic that you'll hit your goal! But as we said above, this isn't just about the number of words you write; it's also about practicing the writing process, which includes finishing what you started. So it's excellent that you're on track to meet your word-count goal, but be sure to find a way to your story's ending as well. Here are a few options to consider:

Wrap it up, wrap it up. Need to hasten your ending? Wipe everyone out with a new highly contagious bacterial disease. Boom. End of story. Or throw some dragons in to swoop down and save your stranded protagonist. Boom. End of story. These are some examples of deus ex machina—a plot device (with a cool-sounding name) you can use to zap seemingly unsolvable or challenging conflicts, thus bringing a story to a close. While deus ex machina can be a quick fix, it doesn't necessarily make for the best ending. Good thing you're going to revise and edit later!

Keep going! Your deadline is up at the end of the week, but you still have energy and you want to push your novel to the end! Great—go for it. Just make sure to give yourself a new deadline (the following week?) so that you actually finish it. Otherwise, you may find yourself working on it for the rest of your life. . . .

Whether you meet your goal or not, the important thing is that you give your story an ending. Because as *Foxfire* author Joyce Carol Oates said, "'The first sentence can't be written until the final sentence has been written.' Only when you have completed a novel, or a story, can you return to the beginning and revise or rewrite."

Plan Your Victory Dance

Get those invitations out to your friends and family, and start practicing your victory party dance moves! Completing a novel in a month (or any writing project in a set amount of time) is a serious cause for celebration, so be sure to find a way to honor your dedication and awesome achievement!

DARE ⚡ MACHINE

Monday: After all of this action, your protagonist pauses and looks in the mirror. What do they see? What do they think?

Tuesday: Your protagonist had a really bad morning. What happened? Or your protagonist had an amazing morning. What happened?

Wednesday: Your protagonist might be feeling a lot of stress at this point in your story. How is that expressed? Do they yell at someone? Hide from everyone? Bite their nails until their fingers bleed? Write a scene that shows how your character deals with the tension.

Thursday: Set a timer for 15 minutes and then describe where your protagonist is (their current location), using as many sensory details as possible.

Friday: One of your characters finds a diary. What's in it?

Saturday: Reread the last page of your favorite book. Did the ending make you cry? Laugh? Feel satisfied? Confused? Think about how it made you feel and why. How do you want your readers to feel at the end of your story?

Sunday: Write two drastically different endings for your story.

WRITER'S ☕ LAIR

Word Count Update

Grab your progress tracker and update it for the very last time! Now go and frame it because it's a beautiful representation of your dedication.

Rearview Mirror

Wow! What an adventure this has been. You set an audacious goal, and then you tackled it with fervor. Take a minute (or a few days) to bask in the afterglow of triumph. Then take some time to reflect back on your experience. How have you changed over the past month? Are you a stronger writer? Are you more confident, and less afraid to get started on big projects?

However you've grown, however you're feeling, you are now an author. Congratulations!

4
Now What?

You did it! You braved the page and made it through your epic writing adventure! You wrote "The End," flicked that last bead of sweat from your forehead, and collapsed onto your bed (possibly for days). So . . . now what? Learn what to do after you complete your writing project draft, including how to revise, edit, and create and keep a writing habit all year long.

⇒ PEP TALK ⇐
by Daniel José Older

Hey, you did it! You finished the story you were writing! That is a gigantic accomplishment, and the first and most important thing you can do is celebrate. That, of course, means something different to everyone, but in this case, it especially means acknowledging that you've accomplished *something*. Not just something—something *difficult*. You worked hard, tussled with ideas and opinions and possibilities; you took time away from whatever else you had on your plate to get it done; you turned a bunch of scattered thoughts into something cohesive. This is no small task. It's much easier to *not* finish. And yet we often run roughshod over the celebrating part and jump right into worrying if the story is any good, if our friends will like it, whether it'll ever get published, yada yada. All that stuff matters, sure, but it's crucial that we pause, reflect on what we've done, and take a moment to appreciate ourselves for doing it. If we don't, we risk making the whole process an endless trudge of self-flagellation and unnecessary hardship. And let's be honest: writing is hard enough as it is without turning yourself into your own worst enemy along the way.

So celebrate. That might mean doing whatever it is you do to relax. I highly recommend picking something that's not even remotely like writing: take a long, aimless walk, go out with friends, catch a movie. Treat yourself. You earned it.

Another good thing about celebrating is it ties in with Things You Do Once You've Finished. Remember that these are all suggestions. These are things that have worked well for me, but process is a personal journey and it's important to figure your own out.

First, you put the manuscript down for a little while and let it breathe. This is important and it can be hard. I know when I finish something, the first thing I want to do is have people read it so I can hear how it sounds or see if it worked or just TALK ABOUT IT BECAUSE IT'S BEEN IN MY HEAD FOR SO LONG AND IT'S FINALLY OUT,

OMG! Okay, yeah, see: it can be a lot, this writing thing—a lot of emotions, a lot of ideas—and that's why it's good to let them simmer after you get them on the page. Often, something super obvious that should be changed will occur to me 24 hours after I finished what I was working on. There's just a part of the creative process that our brain goes through when it's at rest that's different from when it's hard at work.

Okay, so you've celebrated, you've put the project aside for a while. What now? Now comes (cue the horror movie music) EDITS! GAH!! REVISIONS!! Okay, I'm being dramatic. They're not *that* bad. In fact, many writers love revising way more than writing. Edits make me want to throw my computer out the window. Whatever end of the spectrum you're on, though, edits are an unavoidable part of the process. There is no skipping it. There are no shortcuts. Your road to writing always leads to the process of editing. People often don't realize how collaborative a process publishing is. That collaboration is a good thing—it makes our stories better and saves us a lot of time and trouble down the road by catching typos, plot holes, and other embarrassing mistakes before the rest of the world sees our work.

So whether you're getting feedback from your writer's group, fellow students, a teacher, some friends, or a professional editor, or even just going off your own thoughts after you've taken some time away (that shouldn't be the *only* feedback you're getting, though), it's a good idea to embrace the revision process. BUT—and this is important—embracing the process doesn't mean embracing every single note or edit you're given. That would, first of all, be impossible, because some of them may very well be contradictory. But also, some of them will just not be the right advice for your story.

The question I always ask myself with feedback is this: Does the suggested change bring the story closer to its own heart? If it does, I go with it. If it doesn't, I don't. Then we have to ask ourselves what the heart of our story is, and that, of course, is no easy question, and it has no easy answer, but it's the right question to be thinking through. Usually, the heart of a story is not something we can spit out in a simple, flashy sentence and tie up with a nice little bow. That's why it takes the whole story to get at it! It's something you may not be able to articulate clearly at all, but usually you can *feel* it. And that means you can feel when you start to stray from it. It's like a compass. It takes trial and error to learn how to navigate with it, how to discern between the discomfort that means you've taken a wrong turn and the discomfort that means you're growing as a writer (that one you should lean into). But if you put your mind to it, it will become a natural part of your process.

Now you've celebrated, you've let the story rest, you've gathered feedback and sifted through which notes you're going to keep and which you don't need. For me, this is a moment when setting up a clear procedure becomes very important. Edits can feel very hazy and chaotic—you change something here, delete a paragraph there, move some stuff around. Everything you do creates a ripple through the rest of the story, so one change might cause five others. That can make the whole process feel never-ending. (This is the part where I throw my computer out the window.) For me, the solution comes in laying out how things will go as clearly as possible:

- ⟫ Read the whole thing back over.

- ⟫ Read the editorial feedback again.

- ⟫ Make a checklist of the changes I'm going to make. (I like lists! Don't judge me!)

- ⟫ Go through making the bigger changes, responding to what are called the *global notes*.

- ⟫ Go through again, fixing all the small stuff.

- ⟫ Do one more read-over, this time out loud.

See? Now there's a clear path with steps to follow, and even if, in the midst of that, there are moments that feel like slowly falling into a black hole or running through a mirror maze with a thousand clones of yourself speaking different languages, at least you'll have some sense of the bigger picture and where you fit into it.

Lastly, try to find some way to enjoy whatever part of the process you dread the most. For me, obviously, it's editing. So I know that means I have to make extra sure I have a good cup of coffee and terrific music ready for my work session that day. It's the little things that count. Have fun! (*throws computer out window*)

....

DANIEL JOSÉ OLDER is the *New York Times* bestselling author of the young adult series The Shadowshaper Cypher, the Bone Street Rumba urban fantasy series, and the middle-grade historical fantasy *Dactyl Hill Squad*. He won the International Latino Book Award and has been nominated for the Kirkus Prize, the Mythopoeic Award, the Locus Award, the Andre Norton Award, and the World Fantasy Award. *Shadowshaper* was named one of *Esquire*'s 80 Books Every Person Should Read. You can find his thoughts on writing, read dispatches from his decade-long career as an NYC paramedic, and hear his music at his website danieljoseolder.net, on YouTube, and on Twitter @djolder.

BACK TO THE
BEGINNING!

I have rewritten—often several times—
every word I have ever published. My
pencils outlast their erasers.
> —Vladimir Nabokov, *Speak, Memory*

NaNoWriMo participants often ask "Now what?" after they've finished their month of writing with abandon. It's a good question! Here's what we suggest:

First, you celebrate. Sometimes people who haven't written a novel might not understand the enormity of your achievement, so you might want to drop a few hints to your parents to encourage them to treat you to some of your favorite things as a reward for your moxie and grit. You might say something like, "Mom and Dad, remember the ____ I've been wanting to do? I finished writing a novel, even though I'm just a kid, so I was thinking . . ."

Then, after you've treated yourself and done a victory dance (one that involves lots of yelling and shrieking and jumping up and down), you have to decide what you're going to do with your completed draft. Do you want to put it in a drawer to collect dust or bury it deep inside your computer where no one will ever see it (unless you have a nosy little brother or a snooping parent)? Or do you want to unleash your Inner Editor and begin the process of chiseling and reshaping your story so that it's the best it can be?

It might sound like we're pushing that second option, but the first one is just as viable, especially if you wrote your draft solely as an exercise or a way to practice writing. (We recommend not trashing your draft completely, though. You might not think so now, but it could be something you want to revisit in a few weeks, or months, or when you're old and gray and reminiscing about the good ol' days.)

If you're excited about your draft and want other people to read it, or if you're considering publishing it, you'll need to go with the second option;

in other words, you'll need to revise and edit your draft so that it's the best story it can be. (You can also share it before you fix it up, both to get feedback and to show it off!)

The bad news? You'll have more work to do. The good news? Revising and editing can be fun! When you drafted your novel, you built a playground—and now you get to play in it. You and your Inner Editor get to swing across the monkey bars of your plot, transform dull passages into sparkling sandcastles, and slide down sentences, fixing errors as you go. That sounds like a good time, right?

If you're thinking, "Nah, I worked *really* hard on my story, so it's basically perfect already!" we have news for you: a first draft is never a final draft. Ever. Every book on your shelf (or on any shelf!) has been revised and edited, likely many times.

"But wait!" you might object. "You said spelling and grammar didn't matter! You said to write as fast as possible, and to use as many words as possible! Now you're saying those things matter?"

Yes, it's true, we did say all of those things! But we were referring to your *first draft*. Your first draft is about getting from the first word to the last, and the second (and third and fourth) draft is about making sure all the words in between are coherent, spelled correctly, and interesting.

Revision and Editing

Writing a first draft is like being on a high-speed train: the scenery whips past your window, all a blur, trees and buildings and people and cars smooshed into one big, colorful streak. But when the train comes to a stop, the world comes back into focus. The smear that whooshed by when the train was moving becomes a ladybug crawling across a leaf and the individual cracks crisscrossing down the pavement. Revision and editing happen when the train stops; it's then that you can pause and really look at what's in front of you.

Sometimes *revision* and *editing* are lumped together or even used synonymously. But technically, they are two different tasks:

Revision is when you focus on the content and look at the story as a whole; like a camera lens, you zoom out so you can see far and wide. Seeing your entire story helps you fix plot holes and character flaws and tie up loose ends that were missed.

Editing is when you zoom in and focus on the details. When you edit, you go word by word and line by line, fixing spelling and grammatical errors, replacing weak verbs with strong ones, and adding new paragraphs where they're needed.

Revision comes first and then editing. Why? Because if you spend a lot of time correcting spelling and grammar only to find you need to cut an entire section in order for the story to make sense, you're going to feel a wee bit annoyed.

● REVISION

If you pull apart the word *revision* into its prefix and root, you get *re* and *vision*. *Re* means "once more" or "anew," and *vision* means "the state of being able to see." So the revision stage of writing is literally the stage where you get to see your work again afresh.

One of the hardest and most important parts of the revision process is seeing your story through new eyes. You might think your protagonist's best friend is a fully developed, complex character, and maybe she is, but when you reread your novel, you may see that she makes fun of one of her classmates in the beginning of the book, which is something she would *never* do, something that doesn't align with who she is as a person. Looking at your story from a new perspective gives you the chance to see each character arc, or how each character changes and develops across the span of your book; fix any character flaws; and add in details to make characters more complex or their motivations stronger. When you reread, you're also checking to make sure the story makes sense and you're plugging up plot holes and tying up loose ends.

Revision Strategies

Give yourself a deadline. Yes, the deadline's mighty powers extend beyond first drafts. Giving yourself a set amount of time to revise your story will keep you accountable and on track.

Read your story from start to finish, using the revision questions below as a guide. Or read your story several times, and look for a specific thing with each reading.

Make an outline (or if you already made one, take it out and make changes to it if necessary) and use it to check for missing scenes, plot holes, and loose ends.

As you're revising your work, ask yourself these questions:

 Does the beginning of the story pull readers in?

 Is the story's point of view clear?

 Does the order of scenes or events make sense?

 Are there any scenes or events that should be added in?

 Are there any scenes or events that should be removed?

>> Does the story have a clear climax?

>> Does the story have a clear resolution?

>> Are there any major plot holes? (Are there any inconsistencies or things that would never— or could never—happen in the story?)

>> Are all loose ends tied up and resolved?

>> Is there an obvious protagonist?

>> Is it clear what the protagonist wants more than anything?

>> Does the protagonist change over the course of the story?

>> Is there a clear antagonist?

>> Is it clear what the antagonist wants more than anything?

>> Are the main characters multilayered and complex just like people are in real life?

>> Are the main characters' motivations clear? (Is it clear why they do the things they do?)

>> Can you picture what each main character looks like?

>> Does the story have a good balance of action, description, and dialogue?

>> Does the story make sense?

 EDITING

When you edit your story, you're like a bird that's scavenging for insects, only the insects are things like typos, grammatical errors, and poor word choice. These may seem like trivial details, but imagine if the first sentence in *Harry Potter and the Sorcerer's Stone* was, "Mr and Mrs Dursley of number for Privet Drive wer prowd to say that they were perfectly normal thank you very much." That sentence is very difficult to understand because it's riddled with spelling errors and lacks punctuation. Thankfully, authors and their editors take the time to edit their work! So if you want other people to read your book, do them a favor and spend time cleaning it up. You worked hard on your story, so give it the edit it deserves.

Editing Strategies

Don't look at your draft as bad or full of mistakes; instead, see it as a piece of work that needs its finishing touches, like a cake that needs to be frosted, or a ceramic pot that's ready to be glazed.

Read your work out loud and listen carefully for errors. You'll be surprised by how different your story sounds when you hear it as opposed to when you read it.

Know yourself as a writer. If you always misspell a particular word, check to make sure that word is spelled correctly in your story. If you're someone who forgets to capitalize proper nouns, go on a proper noun hunt to make sure they're capitalized correctly.

As you're editing your work, ask yourself these questions:

>> Is every word spelled correctly? (And remember, spell-check is helpful, but it won't catch words that are spelled correctly but used incorrectly, as in "Their playing in the field." All of these are accepted English words, but *Their* is incorrect; the sentence should read, "They're playing in the field.")

Are there any punctuation errors? Have I checked capitalization, commas, periods, question marks, and quotation marks?

 Do my sentences begin in different ways? Are my sentences of varying length?

 Are there any run-on sentences or fragments?

Feedback

In addition to looking at your work with new eyes, it's also helpful to have a completely *different* set of eyes look over your story, too. The person (or people) you select to give you feedback will be able to look at it from a different perspective and spot sections that are confusing, find errors you missed, and point out things that aren't working. They won't just give you constructive (meaning helpful rather than negative) feedback, though; they'll also tell you what's great about your story! Receiving feedback, both positive and constructive, helps us grow into better writers.

Here are a few things to know before you hand your story over to someone for feedback:

Be intentional about who you ask. Don't just give your story to anyone who's willing to read it—be thoughtful about who you select. If your older brother is a fantastic writer but has never said a nice thing to you in his entire life, he might not be the best person to critique your work. The ideal person you pick will be thoughtful, supportive, and able to give constructive criticism. Some people who might fit the bill: one of your parents, a good friend, or a teacher.

If possible, print out a copy of your story for the person who's giving feedback. Ask them to write their comments directly on the manuscript and to mark any errors they come across. When they hand it back to you, you'll be able to see their notes and corrections easily. If you're working electronically, ask the critiquer to either track their changes or to be very specific in their comments, so you know exactly what they're referring to.

To make sure your critiquer understands their role, print a list of what you'd like them to look for. You could include everything on the revision and editing lists in the previous section.

Explain the type of feedback you'd like to receive. This is important because if you only receive positive comments like "cool!" and "nice!" you won't have the opportunity to learn and make your writing stronger. Tell the person giving you feedback that you'd like specific criticism, both positive and constructive. Show them what this looks like. For example, positive criticism may be, "The description of the protagonist in the second chapter is so vivid! I could really see what she looks like." Constructive feedback might be, "In Chapter Two, in the second paragraph, I was confused about what the protagonist was doing. At first I thought she was scaling the building, but then I thought maybe she was just *dreaming* that she had scaled the building. I would make this part clearer so your readers understand what's happening."

⇨ PEP TALK ⇦
by Scott Westerfeld

At the end of drafting a novel, I'm usually in need of a laugh, so I return to the very first pages I wrote. It's like looking at photos of myself in middle school: How innocent I was back then! How badly dressed! But what I've gained since those early days isn't so much wisdom (or a better haircut) but perspective. I can see now where things were headed.

Alas, when looking at old pictures, you can't go back and give yourself advice. But with first drafts you can! In that moment before revising begins, you're no longer stuck in the hurly-burly of "What happens next?" and "What's this character's motivation?" You have perspective.

So here's a suggestion: the first day of a revision is the perfect time to outline your novel again. Perhaps we should call it *re-outlining*, or simply *stepping back*.

It's tempting to start just rewriting Chapter

One. But set that aside for a moment and make yourself a *map*, a big-picture view of how the pieces of your novel fit together.

You probably have your old outline. Put that aside, and look at what you wound up actually writing. A complete draft has its own logic. (If it doesn't, maybe you're still drafting.) Clear away those youthful hopes and dreams and look back at where you went wrong.

A lot of rewriting—like a lot of growing up—is simply admitting how clueless you were not so long ago. (Which is why some people never rewrite, and why some people never grow up.)

So start your revision by answering these questions: Which scenes work, and which are clunky? Which characters never took off, and which turned out to be unexpectedly compelling? Which goals that you started with aren't worth pursuing anymore? And what startling new vistas opened up?

In other words, what do you know now that you didn't know then?

Realize how little you knew when you started, appreciate how much smarter you've become, and accept what innocence you've lost. Then make decisions accordingly, even if that means throwing away the obsessions of your younger self.

To throw one more analogy at you, a novel is like a cloud. When you're in the thick of it, its shape is unknowable. But once you've passed through and gained a little distance, it's much easier to see.

Make sure you take a picture before you dive back in.

....

SCOTT WESTERFELD is the #1 *New York Times* bestselling author of the Uglies series, which has been translated into 35 languages; the Leviathan series; *Afterworlds*; *Horizon*; and many other books for young readers. He was born in Texas and alternates summers between Sydney, Australia, and New York City.

Start a Habit and Write Year-Round

There will come a time—and we can say this with absolute certainty because this time comes for every writer, everywhere—when your imagination will be tired or have a cold or just feel like watching a movie, and it will be up to you to drag it, kicking and screaming, back to the page.

As your imagination's boss, your role is to sit with it and teach it to write through the discomfort. And if you do this enough times—write when you feel like it *and* even when you don't—you'll create something called a *writing habit*, which, unlike biting your nails or leaving the lights on when you're not in the room, is a good habit to have.

Here's another thing: just like Newton's First Law of Motion says that an object in motion stays in motion unless an outside force gets in its way, writers who show up to the page day in and day out continue writing until someone or something gets in their way. Your job is to block those obstacles as best you can so that your words stay in motion.

Having finished an entire novel in a month,

you might be thinking, "I *clearly* have a writing habit already—I wrote every day, or most days, for the entire month!" This is true, but keeping the habit going after such an epic endeavor can be challenging.

Here are some tips for creating a writing habit and keeping it going year-round:

For each writing project, remember your deadline and goal. Keep your deadline and goal in sight at all times. Every day, before you begin writing, tell yourself how many words you'll need to write that day, and how many days you have left before your deadline. Your deadline and goal will help you maintain your writing habit.

Follow a routine and have a ritual. Following a routine and having a ritual will help you form—and keep—your writing habit. They don't need to take a lot of time or be fancy in any way; they just need to be something you can do most days. For a routine, give yourself a set amount of time to write each day, and try to write at the same time every day (or most days). And for a ritual, find a way to mark the beginning and end of your writing time. (See the routine section in Part 1 for tips on getting your routine started.)

Show up. Every. Single. Day. (Or most days.) Some days you'll reach—or even go beyond—your daily word-count goal, and other days you might end up writing just a few words. Some days your enthusiasm will be electric, and other days you'll feel like the power's out in your head. The important thing is to show up, because your project won't write itself. If you know your day is going to be busy, write a bit before breakfast, a bit before dinner, and a bit before you go to bed. If you know you write better in the morning, get up early. If you know you write better at night, skip your television show or video game and write instead. You are the only one who can bring yourself to the page. As Toni Morrison said, "A writer is either compelled to write or not. If I waited for inspiration I wouldn't really be a writer." So enjoy the good days, and be proud of yourself for working through the discomfort on the days when words are slow to come. And if you miss a day, that's okay. If you miss two days, that's okay, too. Don't let those gaps between writing sessions suck you into the belief that you're not a writer. If you write, you are a writer. So get yourself back to the page and carry on.

Find your writing habitat. Some people like to write alone, in absolute silence, while others prefer to write in crowded places, surrounded by the buzz and clangor of everyday life. Whether you prefer the library or your bedroom, a coffee shop or the school cafeteria, find a place to write that you can call your own. (But don't let your writing habitat be an excuse for not writing. If the library is closed, find another quiet place where you can get your words down. Being able to write anywhere is an important skill to hone. As E. B. White said, "A writer who waits for ideal conditions under which to work will die without putting a word on paper.")

Find your writing community. Writing can be a lonely endeavor—your head is down, your mind is in your story, your phone is (hopefully) out of reach—but believe it or not, it can also be a social experience where you form friendships and deepen connections. Having a community of writer friends to talk to about your writing projects and to help keep you accountable makes writing more of a team sport than a solitary one. So where can you find this group of like-minded individuals? Your local library is a good place to start. Ask a librarian if there's a young writers group, and if there isn't one, ask if the library would be willing to start one. (If you're feeling shy about asking, you should know that librarians are possibly the friendliest people on earth.) You could also ask your English teacher if they know of any, or if they could look into it for you. Another great option is to sign up for NaNoWriMo's Young Writers Program (ywp.nanowrimo.org). If you're over the age of 13, our forums are a terrific place to connect with thousands of writers between the ages of 13 and 18.

● YEAR-ROUND WRITING

Coming up with different writing projects can be as hard as keeping a writing habit going. To help inspire your writing over the course of the year, here are 12 creative writing project ideas that will keep your fingers tappity-tapping.

January: Letters

Start the new year with a letter a day. Write to family members near and far, friends, old acquaintances, teachers, and children in hospitals (look online for organizations that send cards to hospitalized kids). Tell people what's going on in your life and that you're thinking about them. Bonus points for writing the old-fashioned way—by hand!

February: Essays or Articles

Essays and news articles don't have to be boring!
Bring your creative flair and try writing a short
essay or article each day, or go for one that's longer
and use the entire month to research and draft it.
Some topics to consider: why cat videos are funny;
the worst song in the world; younger siblings are
the best/worst; if I could meet anyone, I'd meet
_____; whether pie is better than cake.

March: Flash Fiction

It's a bird! It's a plane! No, it's flash fiction! Shorter
than a typical short story, flash fiction pieces run
about 100 to 1,000 words, and still include character
development, conflict, setting, and plot. This
month, challenge yourself to write one flash fiction piece a day—and you never know, your collection of tiny stories might develop into something
much bigger down the road.

April: Camp NaNoWriMo

Pack your creative duffel bag and head to Camp NaNoWriMo! This month, you can work on anything you'd like. Pick a writing project (you can look at the other months for inspiration or revise an old project), set a goal (depending on your project, your goal might be based on word count, number of pages, or amount of time per day), and get started!

May: Short Stories

Write one short story a day, or one short story a week. Short stories have character development, conflict, setting, and plot, and typically focus on a single event. To get started, all you need are these words from "The Gift of the Magi" author O. Henry: "I'll give you the whole secret to short story writing. Here it is. Rule 1: Write stories that please yourself. There is no Rule 2."

June: Poetry

Oh, look, it's the sun!
Poetry month will be such fun.
Grab a pen and some paper,
And capture the world around—and
    inside—you.
Explore different types of poems, like
Sonnets, limericks, haikus,
Free verse, narrative, and maybe epics, too.
Your poems needn't rhyme,
But they can if you'd like.
The most important thing
Is that you have a good time.

July: Camp NaNoWriMo

It's Camp NaNoWriMo again! Pitch a tent on the creativity campground and revise an old project or get started on a new one.

August: Scriptwriting

Act 1: Plan your play or film script just like you would a novel: create a cast of characters and give them motivations and conflicts.

Act 2: Write your script.

Act 3: Put on your play, or film your movie, or just relish the accomplishment of writing a script in a month!

September: Journal Writing

Dear Diary (Is it okay if I call you that? *Dear Journal* doesn't have that same je ne sais quoi),

I know you're not going to believe this because in the past I've written one or two entries and then given up, but for this entire month I'm going to write in you *every single day*. I might write about my day at school, a conversation I had with my BFF, or something I overheard on the bus, or perhaps I'll draw pictures and make collages out of photos. The cool thing about this journal? It'll give me lots of ideas for the novel I'm going to write in November!

Love,
Me

October: Novel Prep

You're one month away from National Novel Writing Month, so it's time to start planning! Go back and reread Part 2 to begin the prewriting process.

November: Novel Writing

Clear your calendar and stretch your fingers, because it's National Novel Writing Month! Go back to Part 3 and begin your writing adventure.

December: Revision and Editing

You wrote a novel, so now what? Now you reread Part 4 and then summon your Inner Editor to help you revise and edit your work so that it's sparkling clean.

When all is said and done, the most important thing for you to do is to keep writing. Write because it's something you love to do; write because it's fun; and write because your stories matter, and the world needs them.

ACKNOWLEDGMENTS

Without Chris Baty, there wouldn't be a National Novel Writing Month. In 1999, his brilliance, creativity, and perseverance spawned the challenge that has helped millions of people around the world realize their creative potential. We are incredibly grateful for his devotion and continued support.

We'd like to thank Tavia Stewart for helping to start and grow the Young Writers Program (YWP). Along with Chris Baty, Jennifer Arzt, Dan Duvall, Ellen García, Lindsey Grant, Ellen Martin, Karlyn Pratt, and Russ Uman, she worked tenaciously to give students and educators the tools and resources they need to tackle audacious goals. When the YWP was still in its early stages, Chris Angotti used his passion and leadership to develop the program further. Marya Brennan is now the director of the YWP. Every day, she steers the program toward bigger and better creative waters—we are lucky to have her at the helm.

Each of NaNoWriMo's staff members contributed

to *Brave the Page* in some way. Thank you to Chris Angotti for coming up with the title; Dave Beck and Jezra Lickter for building the new YWP website; Marya Brennan for adding humor and providing helpful suggestions; Shelby Gibbs for dealing with contracts (amongst many other things); Sarah Mackey for being our in-house Harry Potter expert; and Rob Diaz, Heather Dudley, Katharine Gripp, Tim Kim, and Paige Knorr for their ongoing support. We are so fortunate to be a part of this inspiring community that champions creativity and believes in amplifying young people's voices.

Alyssa Alarcón Santo and Wesley Sueker enlivened the book with their brilliant illustrations; we extend boundless thanks to them for their creative contributions.

We thank John Green, Marissa Meyer, Jennifer Niven, Daniel José Older, Danielle Paige, Celia C. Pérez, Jason Reynolds, and Scott Westerfeld for sharing their time and inspirational words, and for enriching our lives with their stories.

We are forever grateful to our agent, Lindsay Edgecombe, who provided guidance, encouragement, and expertise right from the very start. And we were fortunate to have had not one, but two fantastic editors at Viking Children's Books. Thank you to Alex Ulyett for believing in our vision and for his discerning feedback that helped shape *Brave the Page*. And many thanks to Dana Leydig for jumping aboard enthusiastically and navigating us to the very end with her insights and attention. We'd also like to thank the rest of the Viking team, Nancy Brennan, Kate Renner, Krista Ahlberg, and Lizzie Goodell.

Rebecca and Grant would also like to thank their partners (Ellery and Heather) and their children (August; Jules and Simone) for their love and support and humorous antics that often end up sparking story ideas.

The lifeblood of the Young Writers Program is the tens of thousands of young writers and educators who brave the page year after year. We thank each and every one of them for telling their stories—the world really does need them.

(And a special shout-out goes to the following young writers who submitted advice for *Brave the Page*. We couldn't include all of their sage nuggets of wisdom, but that doesn't mean they weren't useful or appreciated. Thank you to Emma, Malia, Ana, Isabelle, Elizabeth, Amy, Skijai, Eston, Abigail, Cassie, Christine, Rose, Emily, Marissa, Robin, Gabi, Alice, Lavanya, Marlene, Arielle, Sara, Paris, Nova, Amber, Faith, Andrea, Beth, Ailun, Sasha, Marie, Milo, Mili, Nicholas, Bianca, Hannah, Brenna, Simon, Quianna, Erin, Elise, Shelby, Faith, Rachel, Emily, Elizabeth, Sophia, Ghazi, Gryphon, Sophia, Stella, Elizabeth, Lillian, Maya, Maykl, Kayla, Lisa, Chase, Kira, Austin, Brenner, Aarush, Elias, Zoe, Rylee, Katelyn, Hannah, Sarah, Madelynn, Ashley, Alyssa, Kira, Gabriella, Grace, Hannah, Emily, Isabella, Maverick, Ridgedon, Maura, Daniel, Zoe, Mataya, Graydon, Zoe, Nika, Evie, Elaine, Lillian, Alexandria, Ashleigh, Michelle, Katie, Ruby, Heidi, Ella, Quintyn, Joy, Rekha, Johnny, Andrea, Mila, Naomi, Casey, Megan, Anne, Anna, Karoline, Cate, Emily, Rowan, Emily, Yashvee, Hayley, Annika, Camlin, Sasha, Samiksha, Emily, Thea, Jenna, AunnaMaria, Cate, Hero, Winter, Joan, Emily, Rainwolf, Brock, Leah, Winter, S.J., Kaleigh, Ella, Layah, Tracy, Journey, Kitty, Aubrey, Melina, Eleanor, Larkyn, Abigail, Mia, Jacob, Eliza, Maddie, Solaice, Jakob, Sebastian, Anna, Stanley, and Joelle,

Jordan, Zyrah, Gdkailasree, Ethan, Cade, Altea, Ava, Allison, Emie, Jannah, Leixe, Eleanor, Kylie, Ella, Reilly, Astrid, Reinaegh, Nabeehah, Grace, Elise, Arlene, Ella, Altea, Isabella, Linnea, Julie, Grace, Xavia, Mei, and Shea!)

REBECCA STERN has experienced NaNoWriMo from every angle: she had her students participate in the Young Writers Program when she was a teacher, did a victory dance in the 50K winners' circle, served on the organization's Associate Board, and then was Director of Programs. Rebecca is now their Development Manager. Prior to working for NaNoWriMo, Rebecca was a teacher for a decade and a Senior Digital Editor at Pearson Education. She also co-edited an anthology of essays for kids called *Breakfast on Mars and 37 Other Delectable Essays*. She lives in San Francisco with her husband and son and their geriatric dog.

GRANT FAULKNER is the executive director of NaNoWriMo and co-founder of the online literary journal 100 Word Story. His stories have appeared in dozens of literary journals, and his essays on creativity and writing have appeared in such publications as *The New York Times*, *Writer's Digest*, *The Writer*, and *Poets & Writers*. He is also the author of *Pep Talks for Writers: 52 Insights and Actions to Boost Your Creative Mojo* and *Fissures*, a collection of 100-word stories.

ywp.nanowrimo.org